May 2009

LIKE A
SHEPHERD
LEAD US

To Larry — one of our
shepherds. Thank for your
tending to this flock. Hope
this blesses you and your
work.

From us at the Roby COC

DAVID FLEER & CHARLES SIBURT
Editors

LIKE A SHEPHERD LEAD US

Guidance for the Gentle Art of Pastoring

LEAFWOOD
PUBLISHERS

LIKE A SHEPHERD LEAD US
Guidance for the Gentle Art of Pastoring
published by Leafwood Publishers

Copyright © 2006 by David Fleer

ISBN 0-9767790-4-8
Printed in the United States of America

Cover design by Rick Gibson

For information:
Leafwood Publishers
1648 Campus Court
Abilene, Texas 79601
1-877-816-4455 (toll free)

Visit our website: www.leafwoodpublishers.com

07   08   09   10 / 5   4   3

With gratitude
for all who serve
as shepherds
among God's people

CONTENTS

INTRODUCTION

David Fleer & Charles Siburt

One of us recently visited a congregation to teach and preach. At the close of service one of the church's three elders stood in the pulpit, delivered the announcements, and then said, "I have a statement from one of the elders." The sanctuary went silent. The presiding elder revealed that one elder was resigning.

"This is not a moral issue," the presiding elder assured the congregation; "he's done nothing wrong." He wasn't moving to another community or church.

"He'll remain involved in our congregation's life. He's just stepping down," the statement concluded.

This is not often done. So we approached the resigning elder and inquired, "Why?"

He said there was one reason: he was tired and worn out. He claimed that during his five-year tenure he'd made no headway in the eldership or with the congregation. He thought his service had not made any difference.

We knew the man, the congregation, and the eldership and believed he was mistaken. Yet, he convinced us that he was exhausted and that if he were a preacher he'd already have floated his resume and be preparing for a new beginning. Without option of escape, the elder just quit.

While such a resignation may be unusual, we have heard the desire to "step down" expressed countless times. Endless sacrifice and service without training or resources is a toxic mix and will inevitably result in discouragement, a sense of failure, or burnout.

Crises are never planned and seldom handled with ease. How then, in the midst of such demands, do we find nurture for our own spirits? How can we be theologically proactive, not just reacting to trends and the beliefs of our neighbors? How might we reflectively engage our culture, avoiding an easy accommodation on the one hand and seclusion on the other? This volume speaks directly to church elders in just such pursuits.

Not long ago we were planning a conference for church leaders on one of our college campuses. When we submitted a relatively modest book order to the campus bookstore we were surprised by the manager's response. He said, "Elders don't buy books. Your preachers buy books, but not other church leaders." Unconvinced we pushed through the order. The bookstore manager proved to be a prophet: sales were sluggish.

After some reflection we identified at least one reason for the manager's accurate prediction. While a host of books speak directly to ministers' work and life, from homiletics to counseling and spiritual formation, little shelf space is required for the books written for elders. No wonder elders don't buy the books. They've not been written! What elders collect and read contain conversations they can overhear or advice they can indirectly apply. Seldom are elders the intended audience.

In recent years, we have heard many elders repeat a common theme: "I've been asked to serve my congregation as an elder, but no one has ever taught me how to do that, and there are few resources to help me learn." We have found that many of our finest, most committed church leaders feel fatigued, frustrated, or inadequate for the enormous responsibilities they face.

What can we do for a person who serves and provides for the local church with little formal training? What can we do for a person whose Saturday evenings have long been dominated by lesson planning for the next morning's class and whose Wednesday nights are consumed with meetings? What can we do for the person who loves, nurtures, counsels, volunteers, sacrifices, and prays for the church? What can we do for you, the elder?

In our work in Church Relations at Rochester College and Abilene Christian University we have crafted our departments' vision around one critical word: *service*. We are proactively developing and nurturing connections with Churches of Christ and other Christian fellowships by enabling our academic communities to serve congregational leaders across the country. This book is an essential element of that vision.

In 2000 Abilene Christian University established ElderLink to address the serious needs we have articulated. ElderLink's mission is to equip, encourage, and link those who serve as church elders through collaborative relationships, informative resources, and shared learning opportunities. ElderLink programs are now being offered in Portland, Oregon; Nashua, New Hampshire; Atlanta, Houston, Dallas, and Rochester. Each forum provides a mix of plenary speakers and multiple breakout sessions with presentations by outstanding speakers on a variety of subjects of interest to elders. The content of this volume is born out of the ElderLink ministry.

While of a piece, the book divides neatly into three sections, 1) Spirituality (chapters 1-3), 2) Doctrine and Mediation (chapters 4-6) and 3) Christianity and Culture (chapter 7).

Randy Harris opens the volume with an astute article, "Spirituality for the Busy, Frantic, and Overwhelmed." With characteristic wit and sage-like wisdom Harris claims that "The call of the spiritual life is not to more frantic activity but to peace." And he adds the ironic claim that, "If you are overextended you are under committed." Throughout the chapter

Harris's distinctive voice is discernable in phrases like, "If I take this text seriously, what would I have to change in my life? Suddenly the text got very interesting again." Harris's teaching is attractive to both undergraduate college students and church elders alike. One reason, we believe, is the honest and clear notes he sounds. This chapter captures all of that as Harris helps elders move from frantic and overwhelmed to what he believes is the church's greatest need: leaders who are "deep people."

Mark Love's contribution, "The Care of Souls: Pastoral Prayer," claims that effective pastoral ministry occurs when elders function as a sign of God's presence. Prayer is the key for this kind of signifying presence. An effective prayer ministry not only brings people to God's throne in the midst of crisis, it leaves bread crumbs, allowing those needing God to find their way back. Preparation that leads to intentionality is a key to effective pastoral prayer. Love's essay is a thoughtful and practical guide to help elders function as prayerful pastoral caregivers.

In the chapter "Soul Care and the Heart of the Shepherd," David Wray examines a healthy development within our churches. Moving away from organizational and administrative domination, some shepherds are prayerfully seeking strategies to provide soul care and spiritual formation for every disciple in their congregation. Instead of allowing budgets, staff management, facility oversight, ministry coordination, and disputable matters to be all consuming, shepherds are concentrating their time and energy on spiritual values found in Scripture. Wray locates a godly job description embedded in Ezekiel 34, which includes strengthening the weak, praying over the sick, binding up the injured, searching for the lost, and bringing back strays. The essay provides theological justification and practical access to the premise: soul care and spiritual formation should be the crucial organizing principle for the church's elders.

Knowing how often church leaders sit next to patient beds and hospital waiting rooms and pray with families in desperate conditions, readers will find themselves "leaning into" Rubel Shelly's essay, "I Was Sick and You Looked After Me: Pastoral Leadership in Ministering to the Sick." This chapter is at once engaging, caring, helpful and rooted in the world imagined in John 9. Shelly begins with Jesus' remarkable displays of compassionate response to humanity's sad plight and finds the case of the man born blind particularly instructive. He maintains that the work of God in this world is not to explain the unexplainable but to help and heal with tender mercies. Shelly calls elders to take the lead in teaching about the Compassionate Shepherd and living out His script. Perhaps most helpful is Shelly's discussion of end of life issues. Moving beyond the recent public debates, Shelly wisely navigates elders through some difficult scenarios.

One of the church's finest theologians provides good thinking on an essential but seldom discussed matter in, "Moving to the Rhythms of Christian Life: Baptism for Children Raised in the Church." Jeff Childers observes that church leaders often feel uncertain about a person's readiness for baptism—especially a child. Our revivalistic heritage assumes the need for crisis conversion and understands baptism primarily as a badge of membership. This very belief places the deep spiritual devotion of young children in tension. Childers notes that Scripture offers a more dynamic understanding of salvation as a communally grounded process of spiritual formation. Based on the premise that the church is preparing its children for baptism when it is training them for the baptized lifestyle, Childers assists elders to use language and practices that incorporate children—in a more healthy way—into the life of the church.

Writing out of the experience of nearly two decades as director of the Straus Institute for Dispute Resolution and as an active church elder, Randy Lowry provides a most practical essay for managing church conflict. Believing that we will never live in a world without difficult moments, Lowry sets out five guidelines for handling crises in ways that bring peace to our most valued relationships. Blending biblical examples (from Paul's approach in Greece to an Old Testament promise for healing) with pragmatic experiences in legal mediation and the resolution of church conflicts, Lowry's chapter will cause readers to exclaim, "That's exactly where we live!"

Greg Stevenson concludes the volume with his riveting essay, "The Church Goes to the Movies: Standing at the Intersection of Christianity and Popular Culture." Stevenson notes that the current conflict between the church and the entertainment industry is ancestor to a long and heated tradition. Yet, the new century is producing unique challenges for the church, especially those associated with technological innovation. As many younger believers are rejecting organized religion while spirituality remains quite popular, Stevenson asks, "How does the church communicate its relevance to the younger generations in a twenty-first century media-saturated culture while avoiding association with the immoral messages that often thrive in that culture?" Using Hebrews 4:11-12 as a theological foundation, Stevenson calls elders to become honest and constructive dialogue partners in the cultural conversation. Identifying misconceptions and offering helpful suggestions, Stevenson concludes that as "the Word of God is living and active" so the church, as the "Word's vehicle," must be willing to move, adapt, and engage in its cultural setting.

Consistent with the goals of a learning community where scholarship and service are highly valued, we hope that this volume will prove to be a worthy resource for leaders in a wide variety of congregations. Rooted in strong biblical theology, written by respected and dynamic teachers, and addressing topics of critical concern, we pray that you will find in this book ministry enriching tools, resources, and insight.

Chapter 1

SPIRITUALITY FOR THE BUSY, FRANTIC, AND OVERWHELMED

Randy Harris

There was a man who once each month would go to a wise and trusted Christian sage for spiritual guidance. But as the time for his monthly appointment drew near he realized he was just too busy for time with the sage. He thought about calling in sick, but to lie so boldly to his spiritual director just seemed wrong. So he decided to keep the appointment, but to offer no problem or issue to discuss and thus make light the work. He arrived on time and after greetings they got right down to business.

"How is your spiritual life?" the sage inquired. The man readily replied, "It's never been better! I really don't have a single significant issue to discuss."

The spiritual guide expressed surprise. "I don't think in all the times we have talked that there has ever been a time when everything was perfect. Maybe we should discuss what you are doing that is making your spiritual life go so well."

Seeing his strategy for short-circuiting the meeting backfire, the man in frustration simply blurted out the truth, "The fact of the matter is, I really don't have time for this tonight. I have a meeting with the elders in a little while and then a Bible study to teach after that. Life isn't always like this but right now I just don't have the time."

The spiritual director replied, "I see. In that case you better run along to your next appointment and we will meet next month when perhaps you won't be quite so busy."

Now it was the general practice of the director to give the man a few verses at each meeting on which to meditate during the month. "Before I go," said the man, "give me my verse for the month."

But the director refused. "You are very busy and I am sure you won't have time to meditate on any verses. If I give you some and you don't get to them you will just feel guilty."

But the man was so insistent that the sage relented and gave him one verse for the month.

"That's it?" inquired the man. "One verse?"

"Well, you are very busy" said the director. Seeing the uselessness of argument, the man said his farewells and left. But his curiosity soon kicked in for he did not recognize the Bible reference he had been given. So when he entered his car he left the door ajar to keep the dome light on and opened his Bible. He located the verse which simply read, "Are you the Messiah or should we wait for another?"

ENOUGH IS ENOUGH!

This is the place to begin any discussion of spirituality for church leaders—a group of people who surely fit the description of being busy, frantic and overwhelmed. Let me say it as clearly as I can: Spirituality cannot be one more task piled on top of people already overburdened with the care of God's flock. Enough is enough! We are not the Messiah. That job, thankfully, has been taken and done extraordinarily well! You and I must quit acting as if the whole of eternity depends on us doing one more job.

The call of the spiritual life is not to more frantic activity. The spiritual life is rather the call to peace. So, as we come to walk more closely with God, the chaos should recede from our lives. We cease to be under the tyranny of frantic business.

When I visited the Church of the Savior in Washington, D.C., the leaders repeated a phrase that has haunted me ever since. "If you are overextended you are under committed." They take commitment so seriously that they believe one can't be committed to thirty different things. So if you are overextended it's virtually guaranteed that you're under committed. I think that is the description of most Christian leaders I know and it is certainly a description of me. Deeper spirituality is not a matter of doing more stuff.

As in all things, the one we call Lord and Master is our example. We have always been a people who search for patterns. It should be natural for us, therefore, to observe the clear pattern of Jesus' life. Consider three texts that occur in three consecutive chapters in the early part of Luke's Gospel.

When the sun was setting the people brought to Jesus all who had various kinds of sickness, and laying his hands on each one he healed them. Moreover, demons came out of many people shouting, "You are the Son of God!" But he rebuked them and would not allow them to speak, because they knew he was the Christ. *At daybreak Jesus went out to a solitary place.* The people were looking for him and when they came to where he was, they tried to keep him from leaving them. But he said, "I must preach the good news of the kingdom of God to the other towns also, because that is why I was sent.." (Lk. 4:40-43)

Yet the news about him spread all the more, so that crowds of people came to hear him and to be healed of their sicknesses. *But Jesus often withdrew to lonely places and prayed.* (Lk. 5:15-16)

One of those days Jesus went out to a mountainside to pray and spend the night praying to God. When morning came, he called his disciples to him and chose twelve of them, whom he also designated apostles. (Lk. 6:12-13)

Three different times Jesus withdrew for extended times of solitary prayer. What happened during those solitary vigils? Look carefully: each of the three passages has a slightly different nuance and each is crucial to the spiritual life of the Christian leader.

In the first passage Jesus is engaged in a great healing ministry. He goes off for the time alone and when he returns the people encourage him to continue doing what he has been doing. But he says he must continue moving on with his preaching ministry because that is why he was sent. In other words, he says "no" to their request. When Jesus is alone with God he finds the clarity to say "no" when appropriate. Of course this is one of the biggest problems for a conscientious leader—the desire to say "yes" to every good work.

The second passage is even more striking. Jesus walks away from needy, hurting people in order to pray. It appears that sometimes prayer is more important than ministry. If we are ever going to pray, we will have to walk away from ministry opportunities because ministry never gets finished. Ministry is ever-present. There is no end to the needs of the people we are called to serve. But sometimes we serve best by walking away for time with *our* Shepherd.

In the final passage Jesus spends a whole night in prayer prior to making the most important decision of his ministry—the appointing of apostles. For Jesus, decision making is not just a matter of calculating pros and cons and weighing in on this or that—it is seeking the mind of the Father who is generous with wisdom.

To simply follow this pattern of Jesus' life would chase a great deal of the anxiety from our leadership. If we would give ourselves permission to pray rather than be engaged frantically in ministry every moment; if we could minister out of God's call rather than the host of obligations placed upon us; if decision making could come out of deep prayer rather than just strategic planning we would find peace in our spiritual lives.

Four Ways to Pray

Taking our cue from Jesus, we need to think about our prayer life differently. In *Armchair Mystic*, Mark Thibodeaux describes four different ways we pray. We might think of them as stages of prayer though we generally don't quit doing one when we start doing another.

1. Talking *at* God. This is Thibodeaux's way of describing rote prayers. It is the first way we learn to pray. "God is great. God is good. Now we thank you for this food."

Rote prayer in the form of the Lord's Prayer, the Psalms or other prayers of Scripture continue to be an important avenue of prayer for many of us. I have found when I don't have any words of my own for what I am feeling, the psalmist often speaks to my heart. So we never completely outgrow rote prayers.

2. Talking *to* God. But at some point rote prayer is not enough. We don't just want to talk *at* God. We want to talk *to* God. We have things of our own we want to say and so we develop a more conversational approach to God. In prayer we express our personal concerns. I don't need to dwell here because this makes up the bulk of our prayer life. Most of us are comfortable talking to God.

The problem is that we often get stuck here. Our prayer life begins and ends with speaking to God. But there is still a longing in us for something more. The one-sidedness of this conversation gets old. Sharing everything with God is a great thing, but we also want to hear from God. We want some guidance in our lives.

3. Listening to God. The third way of praying is learning to *listen* to God. One of the major differences in idol worship and the worship of the living God comes into play at precisely this point. Consider Habakkuk 2:18-20.

> Of what value is an idol, since a man has carved it?
> Or an image that teaches lies?
> For he who makes it trusts in his own creation;
> he makes idols that cannot speak.
> Woe to him who says to wood, "Come to life!"
> Or to a lifeless stone, "Wake up!"
> Can it give guidance?
> It is covered with gold and silver;
> there is no breath in it.
> But the Lord is in his holy temple;
> let all the earth be silent before him.

One speaks to an idol because it is going to say nothing. But in the presence of a living God silence is the first posture. I am not suggesting that with an audible voice in the ear God is going to give us specific instruction on every particular issue about which we have a question. I am asking us to believe what James tells us: "If any of you lacks wisdom, he should ask God who gives generously to all without finding fault, and it will be given to him."

Soon after I concluded my formal graduate education I went to a large church to preach. I had prepared my whole life to be an academic and was reasonably competent in the college classroom. But ministry to this church was a different matter. Since I had been trained in Scripture and theology and done a lot of speaking I preached pretty good sermons from the beginning.

But I did not have the first idea how to love a church or lead a church. Needless to say the first couple of years went rather badly, but the elders were patient and believed I could do it—they saw qualities in me I did not see in myself.

Eventually I made the commitment to start praying over the church for two hours a day, five days a week. I cannot tell you how that transformed my ministry. My pastoral judgment got better, I dealt with people's spiritual lives and problems in more godly ways. Almost nothing ever came up that I hadn't prayed over deeply. God was faithful to his promises as I learned to listen for guidance—he gave wisdom.

Sometimes we are so cavalier with the idea of the listening prayer that we give it a bad name. We have all heard or used the phrase "God has laid on my heart." This statement is sometimes used as the ultimate trump card for getting our own way or justifying our actions. Who can question what God has spoken? But more often such a statement just reflects a lack of discernment because not every nudge or inclination we feel is necessarily the work of the Holy Spirit. We learn to practice discernment in listening prayer: through scripture, the community of faith, and further prayer.

Listening prayer is largely going to be done with the engagement of scripture. We read the Bible but do we really listen to God? Often we find ourselves studying the Bible because we know we ought to and it is supposed to be good for us, but it is not altogether clear we are getting much out of it (especially if we are reading through the Bible and have gotten stuck in Leviticus). In fact there was a time I had gotten really bored with the Bible. I had read it a lot and I was pretty sure I knew what it said and I wasn't learning anything new. Most of my reading was aimed at preparing a sermon or teaching a class or solving a problem.

A friend helped me through this vexing period by suggesting that there is only one really serious Bible study question: If I take this text seriously, what would I have to change in my life?

Suddenly the text got very interesting again. Now I wasn't interrogating the Bible but allowing the Bible to interrogate me. There is a huge difference in asking questions about the Bible and allowing the Bible to call you into question. Scripture has a radical way of looking at things and often confounds our most basic notions about the world.

I started asking, "What's in this text that I don't really want to hear?" Take Jesus' teaching on forgiveness for example. How many times must I forgive—seven times? I must confess that granting forgiveness seven times sounds pretty generous (if you are in my class you won't get seven!). But Jesus says seventy times seven. Jesus seems to be saying that we offer forgiveness not on the basis of the worthiness of the other person but on the way God has forgiven us—even when we get to the point where the other person seems really undeserving. I have a difficult time forgiving people when I think they deserve it, much less when I am sure they don't. So the text confronts us and asks whether we are going to take this seriously enough to bring our lives into conformity with it. At this moment our reading Scripture becomes not just *informative* but *transformative*.

I sometimes think we try to read too much Scripture—we see how much of it we can get through. The rapid reading of text to acquire information has its usefulness. We sometimes see a gospel or an epistle with new clarity when we read the book from beginning to end in one sitting. But there is another way of reading, often called *lectio divina* or "divine reading," where we read a very short passage and then just meditate and chew on it until it becomes part of us, and then we are transformed by it.

It is highly unlikely that we will be spiritual teachers if we have ceased to be spiritual learners—what Scripture would refer to as disciples. Engaging the Bible in a transformative way does not require *more time* in study but a different *attitude* as we come to the text—a humility and willingness to be changed more into the likeness of Christ. To do this and then teach others this relationship with God's Word is a major part of what it means to be both a disciple and leader.

4. Being with God. But there is one other way of praying. To understand this last way, think about your most precious human relationships. Undoubtedly they have been filled with rich events and conversations. But, in these most valued experiences language is sometimes unnecessary and can even interfere. Some of your richest times with the ones you most love are when you are not trying to accomplish anything. You may not even be speaking—you are just spending time with the one you love.

This fourth way of praying is like that—it is just *being with* God. Klaus Issler describes this experience with the wonderful phrase "wasting time with God." Of course such time is no more wasted with God on these occasions than it is with that loved one. But it does convey the message that this is not about getting anything from God—it is just hanging out with the one you love. This kind of prayer becomes a little vacation with God each time we do it—no agenda, no demands, no expectations.

I am constantly amazed at how even a few minutes of intentionally coming into God's presence can transform our lives. I taught a class recently that I frequently found exasperating. Though my students were wonderful people they were very immature! (Am I getting old?) I found myself often frustrated and short-tempered. I started spending the ten minutes right before I went to class with God in prayer. I don't think I prayed for anything in particular but I was getting re-oriented to my true self—and a desire to be the same person when with my students. It was amazing the difference that made.

These four ways of praying have a common purpose that goes beyond what we normally think of as prayer. The point is for us to be so conscious of the presence of God in our lives and in our own world that even when we aren't praying we are living out this awareness. When we live in the presence of God all of life becomes a kind of prayer to God.

LEARNING TO BE WITH GOD

To help us learn to live in God's presence, consider Elijah's experience *after* his victory on Mount Carmel. Elijah is on the run from Jezebel who has threatened assassination. He flees to Horeb, which we know better as Sinai, for this is the one place he is sure God will be present with him. And here we have one of the strangest stories in the Old Testament.

> And the word of the Lord came to him: "What are you doing here, Elijah?" HE replied, "I have been very zealous for the Lord God Almighty. The Israelites have rejected your covenant, broken down your altars, and put your prophets to death with the sword. I am the only one left, and now they are trying to kill me too."
>
> The Lord said, "Go out and stand on the mountain in the presence of the Lord, for the Lord is about to pass by."
>
> Then a great and powerful wind tore the mountains apart and shattered the rocks before the Lord, but the Lord was not in the wind. After the wind there was an earthquake, but the Lord was not in the earthquake. After the earthquake came a fire, but the Lord was not in the fire. And after the fire came a gentle whisper. When Elijah heard it, he pulled his cloak over his face and went out and stood at the mouth of the cave.
>
> Then a voice said to him, "What are you doing here, Elijah?"
>
> He replied, "I have been very zealous for the Lord God Almighty. The Israelites have rejected your covenant, broken down your altars, and put your prophets to death with the sword. I am the only one left, and now they are trying to kill me too."
>
> The Lord said to him, "Go back the way you came, and go to the Desert of Damascus. When you get there, anoint Hazael king over Aram. Also, anoint Jehu son of

Nimshi king over Israel, and anoint Elisha son of
Shaphat from Abel Meholah to succeed you as prophet.
Jehu will put to death any who escape the sword of
Hazael, and Elisha will put to death any who escape the
sword of Jehu. Yet I reserve seven thousand in Israel—
all whose knees have not bowed down to Baal and all
whose mouths have not kissed him." (I Kings 19:9b-18)

God first questions Elijah's purpose for being there. Then
God shows Elijah all sorts of powerful manifestations although
God is not in any of them. Finally God orders Elijah off the
mountain and tells him to get back to work. What is God trying
to teach Elijah here? I think the narrator's point is this: God is
not just present in special places and significant events like
Carmel or Sinai; he is also present in the everyday routine of our
lives and ministry.

This truth is fundamental to our spiritual well being. As
important as moving times of prayer and inspiring worship services are, we must come to experience the presence of God in
all of life including the utterly mundane. This is the definition of
spiritual maturity: the ability to see God in all things.

Perhaps you have read *The Prayer of Jabez* (not the prayer
in the Bible but the book). Many critical things can be said
about the book. For one, it has little to do with the text on
which it is based—the passage is doing something quite different than is the author of the book. For another, all the
examples in the book tend to be triumphalistic which is a
major problem because we all know people deeply committed
to ministry who have hammered away on stony soil for years
and years and never experienced the kind of success the book
talks about.

There is, however, an absolutely life-transforming idea in
The Prayer of Jabez. The book asks us to consider what life
would be like if we went through our day asking God to give

us more ministry. Now that is a great way to live. What would happen if we went through a day asking God, "Is there a kingdom possibility in this moment? What kind of ministry can happen right now?"

I have occasionally put *The Prayer of Jabez* approach to the test. Following a cue from the author, I often do it in airports. I spend a lot of time in airports where one often sees people at their worst. When things go smoothly in an airport everyone takes it for granted but when things go badly most people take it personally. So from time to time I will say to God, "Okay, I'm going to be here an hour (I hope). I'm never going to see these people again. In the next few minutes give me some ministry. Let me join you now in doing a little something for your kingdom."

Strange as it may sound, something always happens. Now I don't believe that in response to my prayer God walks up behind someone and shoves them in my direction. I think the effect is more on me. That is, at that moment I am placing myself at God's disposal and seeing the world through God's eyes. In a world as hurting and broken as ours, kingdom possibilities are all around us. If only the scales would fall from our eyes we could see.

At Abilene Christian University where I teach, hundreds of our students go on Spring Break Campaigns. They go all over the United States and even out of the country for a week of ministry rather than to the beach in Florida. All of the groups know their destination well in advance except for one campaign group with which I have occasionally worked. This group is called "Seek and Follow." They believe you don't have to have a strategic (or non-strategic for that matter) plan to serve God; all you need is openness to his leading. So they pray and go with no fixed destination in mind but eyes and hearts searching to do ministry.

Then they come back with their glowing report. "Let us tell you what happened! We went to such and such a place and when we got there they were in desperate need of us and we had just enough people to do the job and then we went to the next place and it happened again and we just know God was leading us all the way!"

And I respond to them, "I think God was leading you, too, I just don't think he was leading you in the way you think he was. Is it possible God was speaking in one of your ears at every crossroad, telling you where to go? God has done it before and done stranger things, too. But, in a world like ours you could have gone in any direction, any number of miles and anywhere you stopped would have been a place you were desperately needed. You went out with your spiritual antenna up and everywhere you went you were asking, 'What does God want to do here? What are the kingdom possibilities at this time in this place?' With that openness of heart you saw the opportunities that are around you every moment of every day." Through the habits of listening to God and being with God we can become sensitive to God's purposes all around us.

This is what Brother Lawrence meant with the title of his book, *Practicing the Presence of God*. We look for God not just in the obvious "religion" moments but in life's events, too. The glorious thing about this is that it requires *no* time. We do not see ministry as one more activity piled on top of all the others; everything we are already doing becomes ministry. Those who have been involved in ministry for a while know how true this is: Often the most important ministry we do is while we are on the way to do what we thought was the important ministry.

At the close of each school year we have what we call a "senior blessing" for all the graduating seniors from the Department of Bible, Missions, and Ministry. During that time the students often share their most meaningful experiences from the previous four years and more often than not it is not something that happened in a class or formal worship setting; it is a personal encounter that happened in a home or office or hallway.

This way of being in the world doesn't just happen—it has to be cultivated. As God warned Israel, "When you get into the

Land of Promise…don't forget me!" So we need an occasional warning: in our lands of promise don't forget the presence of God (Deut. 6:10-12). The greatest problem in our spiritual lives is simple forgetfulness. We go through large portions of our days without giving God much thought, and thereby miss the fullness of each moment and possibilities for ministry.

I have been involved in several disastrous elders' meetings when I have not "practiced the presence of God." I've been pre-occupied with my own agenda. If, however, we'd asked, "What does God want to happen with us?" or "What is God trying to do here," the outcome would have been radically different.

Spiritual leadership might simply be called God-awareness. Spiritual leadership is seeking the spiritual dimension in all things. All other kinds of prayer and spiritual discipline that we practice are aimed at deepening this moment-by-moment awareness of God's presence.

DRIVING DRIVENNESS AWAY

I want to conclude with a word of encouragement based in a deep theological truth. Many of the church leaders I encounter are tired and discouraged. They have discovered what we all find out eventually: we are in over our heads. We are hopelessly inadequate to our task; we fail more often than we succeed. And then we find ourselves getting cynical.

Spiritual leaders ought to be joy-filled dreamers. Few things are more destructive of spiritual life than cynicism. Cynicism is a sin that needs to be rooted out of our lives. It is a failure of the Christian imagination and faith in what God can do in our world. Romans 8:18-28 is the classic counter to cynicism and points to our source of hope for living in this world.

> We know that the whole creation has been groaning
> as in the pains of childbirth right up to the present time.
> Not only so, but we ourselves, who have the firstfruits

of the Spirit, groan inwardly as we wait eagerly for our adoption as sons, the redemption of our bodies. For in this hope we were saved. But hope that is seen is no hope at all. Who hopes for what he already has? But if we hope for what we do not yet have, we wait for it patiently....And we know that in all things God works for the good of those who love him, who have been called according to his purpose.

This passage encourages us to take seriously the fact that all of creation is groaning while it waits. The twin towers fall and the world groans. The hurricanes strike and the world groans. Not only does the world groan but the children of God also groan while we wait. We sin and falter and fail—and we groan. Even the Holy Spirit groans in this passage.

But this travail is a groaning in hope that is giving birth to a new creation of God's love against which no power can stand. And in the midst of this groaning world we are told God is working in all things for his children and this is our hope—that whatever happens, good or bad, God *incorporates* it into his glorious plan, the redemption of all creation.

This does not mean that everything that happens is a direct act of God or that everything that happens is good but that God can work in all things. I was impressed not long ago in a mentoring group of young men training for ministry, when I asked them to tell me what they wanted to do with their lives. A third of them said something to do with mission in predominately Muslim lands. Prior to 9/11 those countries weren't even on our radar screen. Out of the rubble of that disaster God raises up new missionary commitment to a neglected part of the world—for God works in *all* things.

We have seen divorced people who minister mightily to those whose families are breaking up. We have witnessed recovering addicts who are God's vessel for rescuing others caught in addiction. Divorce and addictions are not God's will, but even in brokenness God works.

Among the Christian leaders (particularly elders) whom I meet, spiritual difficulty is exasperated by frustration and fatigue. Yet, we understand that in the end God will accomplish all that God has purposed. So, at the very moments we seem to be getting nowhere and the powers of darkness appear to be winning the day, we might remind ourselves that God works in all things and God cannot be thwarted. Not by our wisdom, our work, or our righteousness but by God's love and power ministry will be completed.

So it is possible for us to go to bed at night, no matter what kind of day it has been, and sleep. As Thomas Kelly puts it,

> Life from the Center is a life of unhurried peace and power. It is simple. It is serene. It is amazing. It is triumphant. It is radiant. It takes no time, but it occupies all our time. And it makes our life programs new and overcoming. We need not get frantic. He is at the helm. And when our little day is done we lie down quietly in peace, for all is well.

At the time in his ministry when things had never been worse, Paul was reassured by his conviction that the power of God which raised Jesus from the dead was also working in him, even when it was hard to see or believe.

> We do not want you to be uninformed, brothers and sisters, about the hardships we suffered in the province of Asia. We were under great pressure, far beyond our ability to endure, so that we despaired even of life. Indeed, in our hearts we felt the sentence of death. But this happened that we might not rely on ourselves but on God, who raises the dead. He has delivered us from

such a deadly peril, and he will deliver us. On him we have set our hope that he will continue to deliver us. (2 Cor. 1:8-10)

Glenn Hinson argues that what the church needs most are saints—people who have truly placed their lives under God's will and control. We don't just need leaders with greater skill, we need leaders who are deep people. Do you hear the call to lead out of your own deep spiritual life?

If we learn to pray the way Jesus prayed, read the Bible in a transforming way, practice God's presence in the everyday routine of life, and catch the vision of the God who works in *all* things, we can be the deep leaders the church needs. And in the process we will discover that true spirituality is not one more activity to add to overburdened lives but a way of living that drives our drivenness away. Then we discover the blessedness to lead without guilt and that the promise of Jesus rings true—the yoke is easy and the burden is light.

BIBLIOGRAPHY

Brother Lawrence. *Practicing the Presence of God.* New Kensington, PA: Whitaker House, 1982. A little book by a monk exploring the question of whether God can be experienced in the midst of such mundane activities as washing the dishes and hoeing the garden.

Foster, Richard. *Celebration of Discipline: The Path to Spiritual Growth.* New York: HarperCollins, 1978. The best "how to" book on the traditional spiritual disciplines from a contemporary Quaker with a study guide also available. Very accessible.

Holloway, Gary, and Earl Lavender. *Living God's Love: An Introduction to Christian Spirituality.* Siloam Springs, AR: Leafwood Publishers, 2004. A simple and practical introduction to the spiritual disciplines, especially suitable for members of Churches of Christ.

Hinson, E. Glen. *Spiritual Preparation for Christian Leadership*. Nashville, TN: Upper Room, 1999. A call by the foremost Baptist scholar of spirituality in our century for leaders not just to be managers but deep spiritual people.

Kelly, Thomas. *A Testament of Devotion*. New York: Harper & Brothers, 1941. The greatest book of Quaker spirituality of the 20th century, this book is a welcome antidote to our often chaotic approach to our spiritual lives.

Nouwen, Henri. *The Way of the Heart: Desert Spirituality and Contemporary Ministry*. New York: Seabury, 1981. A tiny book that changed my life and that I continue to read over and over. A profound call to silence, solitude and prayer by a Catholic spiritual master of the contemplative life.

O'Connor, Elizabeth. *Call to Commitment: The Story of the Church of the Saviour, Washington, D.C.* San Francisco: Harper & Row, 1963. Tells the story of the Church of the Savior in Washington, D.C., which in my estimation does a superb job of combining the inner life and the outer life of engagement.

Ortberg, John. *The Life You've Always Wanted: Spiritual Disciplines for Ordinary People*. Grand Rapids, MI: Zondervan, 2002. A wonderfully written, accessible (though not very deep) exploration of the rationale for and practice of spiritual disciplines.

Thibodeaux, Mark. *Armchair Mystic: Easing into Contemplative Prayer*. Cincinnati, OH: Saint Anthony Messenger, 2001. The best introduction to listening prayer and contemplative prayer I know. Wonderful suggestions and exercises to get started. A must for those wanting to pursue the discipline of listening prayer.

Thompson, Marjorie. *Soul Feast: An Invitation to the Christian Spiritual Life*. Louisville, KY: Westminster John Knox, 1995. Another wonderful introduction to the spiritual disciplines with discussion questions and exercises that make it ideal for classes or small groups. Covers some things other books don't, like hospitality and a rule of life.

Willard, Dallas. *The Spirit of the Disciplines: Understanding How God Changes Lives*. San Francisco: HarperSanFrancisco, 1990. A must read book. The subtitle says it well: "understanding how God changes lives." The best book on why (rather than how) the spiritual disciplines make sense. Not the easiest reading but well worth the effort.

Chapter 2

THE CARE OF SOULS

Pastoral Prayer

Mark Love

Elders are asked to attend to the most intimate concerns in ways that convey the active presence of God. Parents agonize over the fate of their son who has fallen in with the wrong crowd and only comes home when he needs money. A man becomes so driven by performance in his work that all other matters become secondary, including his family and spiritual life. A young mother wastes away in a hospital bed as cancer ravages her body. Two church members live in open conflict over disagreement about discipline policy for the Sunday School. A husband confesses that his temper is out of control and that it has harmed his family. Gossip harms a new Christian with a checkered past. In these situations, and countless others, elders are often asked to represent God to persons in the midst of trouble. No greater work occupies the attention of the elder than the care of souls.

As with all work of great significance, the care of souls carries both promise and peril. To witness the transformation of a life, or to see life come out of death, or to watch lives become reconciled to God and to one another is to stand in view of miracle. Still, care of souls is not all promise. Beyond the disappointment and heartache that come when lives do not conform to the will of God, the care of souls invites potential abuses of power and spiritual influence. The stories are legion of well-intentioned elders whose actions poison the soil of spiritual growth and vitality. It is not enough, it seems, to express concern for those in our care. Rather, in Paul's words, spiritual concern must be expressed as the "affection of Christ" (Phil 1:8). It matters that we are present with people and that our presence offers the presence of Christ.

PAUL AND PASTORAL CARE

Paul's goal for each Christian is "Christ formed in you" (Gal 4:20). Yet Paul knows well the risks of pastoral care. He knows that some ways of being present with people work against the goal of pastoral care. Still, he labors with churches so that Christians will grow into the full stature of adult faith, opposing those who would stunt the growth of their spiritual children. Paul contrasts his approach with that of his Galatian opponents:

> They make much of you, but for no good purpose; they want to exclude you, so that you might make much of them. It is good to be made much of for a good purpose at all times, and not only when I am present with you. My little children, for whom I am again in the pain of childbirth until Christ is formed in you.... (Gal 4:17-19)

For Paul, it is possible to "make much" of people, to smother them with concern, and to impair their progress toward God. You and I have witnessed the kind of stifling care Paul critiques. Some have the unfortunate ability to simultaneously make people feel special and inadequate. Like an over-protective mother who can't understand why her adult son never made anything of himself, these overbearing leaders constantly point out all the ways that their "children" are lacking. Constantly taking the temperature of those under their care, these leaders persistently call the faithfulness of others into question. As Paul shrewdly observes, this "making much of" actually serves the purpose of making people feel at risk in their faith. "They want to exclude you so that you may make much of them."

Paul's insightful analysis of his opponents' pastoral interests suggests that this kind of constant attention actually enhances the power interests of those in a position of authority. "They make much of you...so that you may make much of them." For Paul, this runs contrary to a gospel that proclaims strength in weakness. Today, we might criticize Paul's opponents for overfunctioning or for creating co-dependent relationships. Paul's name for their approach is "the way of the flesh," which has nothing to do with the gospel of Christ. In contrast to the manner of the flesh which emphasizes human will and achievement, Paul envisions another style of pastoral care: "the way of the Spirit," which emphasizes faith and freedom. While the way of the flesh ultimately serves the interest of the caregiver, the way of the gospel leaves room for the power of the Spirit. While the way of the flesh begins with an assumption of exclusion, the way of the Spirit begins with the assumption of gracious inclusion. The way of flesh is law-measuring, condemning and trapping. The way of the Spirit requires freedom. The way of the flesh works only through constant and diligent presence. The way of the Spirit works both in presence and absence.

The interplay of presence and absence is important for Paul. His letter to the Philippians underscores this concern. He writes to convince the Christians in Philippi that God will complete the good work begun in them regardless of whether or not he returns to visit them. It is important for Paul that both his presence and absence teach the Philippians not to trust him but God, who "will fully satisfy every need of yours according to the riches of his glory in Christ Jesus" (Phil 4:19). Paul's letter conveys what Fred Craddock calls an "intimate distance."[1] Paul is vitally engaged with the Philippians, but in a way that leaves room for the active presence of Christ.

Henri Nouwen sees a similar rhythm of presence and absence in Jesus' statement to his disciples about his departure and the subsequent coming of the Spirit. Jesus' absence from them will allow for a different, more intimate presence, mediated by the Spirit. Nouwen draws the following pastoral implications from Jesus' words in John:

> I am deeply convinced that there is a ministry in which our leaving creates space for God's spirit and in which, by our absence, God can become present in a new way....
>
> The words of Jesus: "It is for your good that I leave" should be a part of every pastoral call we make. We have to learn to leave so that the Spirit can come. Then we can indeed be remembered as a living witness of God....
>
> Therefore, a sustaining ministry requires the art of creative withdrawal so that in memory God's Spirit can manifest itself and lead to the full truth. Without this withdrawal we are in danger of no longer being the way, but in the way; of no longer speaking and acting in his name, but in ours; of no longer pointing to the Lord who sustains, but only to our own distracting personalities.[2]

In both Paul's letters and Jesus' words to his disciples we see modeled a type of pastoral presence that leaves room for the healing ministry of the Spirit of God.

TRANSPARENT PRESENCE AND PASTORAL CARE

So how do we practice the care of souls while avoiding Nouwen's concern about "being in the way?" How can we be present to people in a way that reminds them of and prepares them for the greater presence of the Spirit? Elders need to be present for people in a way that does not focus on the elder himself. Put another way, effective pastoral ministry occurs when the elder is "transparently present." A transparent presence enables those who experience our care to see through us to God, the true source of our soul's healing. The pastor signifies God's direct involvement through a creative rhythm of presence and absence. Prayer is the key for this kind of transparent presence.

When we pray with others, we are present, but as someone else's representative. Prayer is simultaneously a powerful and submissive act. In prayer an elder brings another's name boldly before the throne of God. But prayer also invites us to our knees in the presence of the Almighty, indicating our submission to someone else's will. Prayer is the elder's way of indicating that the effective presence in pastoral care is not the elder but God himself.

Many things may happen in the course of pastoral care. Advice is given. Problems are analyzed. The Bible is read and discussed. It might be tempting to think of prayer as simply one more thing an elder brings to any given situation. However, prayer is more than just one option in the pastor's toolkit. Prayer is the bedrock of all caregiving offered in the name of Jesus. Elders should not think of themselves primarily as counselors or problem solvers or even as expert teachers. Elders pray. Other roles, while important, are secondary.

Church leaders sometimes think of themselves primarily as problem solvers. Solving other people's problems provides an undeniable sense of usefulness and even power. It is tempting for elders to think of members as spiritual clients whose problems need to be fixed. Defining pastoral relationships in terms of "fixing" others leaves the door open for abuses of relational power. It is one thing to work *with* people, still another thing to work *on* them. Given both the intimacy and vulnerability that often accompany pastoral situations, great care must be taken to define appropriate relationships in pastoral care.

In contrast, defining pastoral encounters primarily in terms of prayer clearly communicates appropriate roles for bringing God's care into the lives of others. It stands to reason, therefore, that intentional preparation for prayer helps to establish a healthy environment for spiritual care. When a distraught parent or injured spouse or disgruntled church member comes for care, elders do well to indicate clearly that prayer will be the focus of pastoral attention. Too often, prayer is a simple formality, an obligation satisfied at the beginning or end of a pastoral visit. With some thoughtfulness and intentionality, however, all that happens in a pastoral visit can be thought of as preparation for prayer. In fact, intentionally preparing for prayer requires skills that are always beneficial in helping people—for example, asking good questions, listening more and speaking less, and exploring possible outcomes. When these aspects of care are pointed intentionally toward prayer, God's presence is both communicated and anticipated.

Intentional preparation for prayer also allows deeper discernment to emerge for both the elder and the person for whom prayer is being offered. Discernment, in turn, yields richer prayer. For instance, if a person battling cancer came to us, we would pray for healing or for God to guide doctors. But seldom do we explore in intentional ways the nature or character of God in relation to this concern. In my experience, asking the "God questions" greatly deepens the prayer experience. Now prayer may move beyond petitions for healing, though these are still important, to a deeper longing to know God as healer. As a result, these prayers model for those in our care how they too might pray on their own behalf and for others. Through prayer a faithful pastor renders space for God's presence in sufficient detail and clarity so that people may, on their own, confidently return.

SETTING THE STAGE: THE PRE-PRAYER INTERVIEW

In my work with the elders of the East County Church of Christ,[3] preparation for prayer became a focus of our pastoral learning. We brought intentionality to pastoral prayer by thinking carefully about the questions that would best prepare us for the ministry of prayer. As a result, we developed a pre-prayer interview. This interview not only laid the foundation for prayer, but also defined the relationship between the shepherd and person receiving care.

The pre-prayer interview accomplishes several purposes. It communicates God's welcome and concern. The questions asked in the interview help clarify the petitioner's interests. Just as important, the interview encourages all who have gathered for prayer to reflect on God's nature and concerns. Through careful listening, the pre-prayer interview allows a strategy to emerge in the overlap of the petitioner's interests and God's nature. That is, as we discern those places where our desires and God's nature overlap, we find focus for prayer. Finally, the pre-prayer interview allows elders to clarify their role which ultimately points to God's presence.

Here is the pre-prayer interview we developed at the East County congregation:

1) *Welcome.* Expressing welcome may seem obvious, but it bears emphasizing. Many fail to seek the care they need due to feelings of shame or embarrassment. Welcome may take many forms and be expressed in many different ways, but an elder must communicate both grace and security.

2) *Why have you come?* Discerning God's will requires a great deal of listening. Those seeking care need to know they can express themselves fully and honestly. Our instincts to move quickly to solutions tend to minimize the unique experience of the one seeking care.

There may very well be a place for correction and exhortation in relation to a pastoral concern, but the first act of preparing for prayer is listening. Questions that seek clarification deepen perceptions of care and attentiveness and invite free speech. "You said that God feels far away. Can you tell me more about that?" or "Tell me more about what you were feeling when you got the news from the doctor."

3) *Why would this concern be something to bring to God?* Who is God in relation to your concern? These questions move the focus from the one seeking care to the nature and character of God. This change in focus is extremely important. Concerns simply look different when God is the reference point. Sometimes we need to be reminded of what we already know about God. Other times our views of God need to be expanded. The burdens we bear are sometimes greater because of inadequate understandings of God's relation to our concerns. Questions about God allow these inadequate views to surface and be tested in conversation. In turn, focus on the nature of God provides hope. As we will see later in this chapter, the psalmists often match their petitions to the nature of God. In other words, psalms seeking God's forgiveness often appeal to God's merciful nature and steadfast love. Those seeking protection address God as a rock or fortress. In this way questions about God allow an elder to frame a prayer strategy within the very nature and character of God.

4) *What is your desired outcome?* Once God's nature has been explored, it is good to imagine outcomes. As with the previous two questions, questions about outcomes move from the petitioner's own desires to reflection on outcomes pleasing to God. Many feel a sense of desperation in relation to their concern because they

cannot imagine a hopeful future. Others have a very definite outcome in mind. Their steely resolve toward only one possible future often blocks the way forward. God can only be seen as active and concerned if their own desired future comes about. Both a lack of imagination with regard to outcomes and a rigid determination about desired results are detriments to God's movement in situations of pastoral care.

5) *What would be a godly outcome to this situation?* This question provides both a corrective to selfish or limited views of the future and emphasizes that God's will can be expressed in different ways. Just as it is important for members to be aware of multiple possible outcomes, so elders need to be open as well. Some problems, particularly those dealing with sinful behaviors, possess only one godly outcome. But many problems can have multiple godly outcomes. In situations like this, elders need to make sure that this is a collaborative and open conversation.

6) *How do you see my role?* Many who come for care have no expectations beyond the moment. However, some have very concrete and unrealistic expectations. It is good to know those expectations.

7) *Here is how I see my role.* Several things need to be communicated to provide a healthy foundation for pastoral relationships. *Confidentiality.* Those things shared with an elder are held in strict confidence and will only be shared with others if permission is granted. This includes sharing with other elders, ministers, or spouses. Confidentiality provides the safety people need to bring struggles into the open. *Persistence in prayer.* Here, the elder communicates clearly the nature of the care being offered. Elders are not counselors. If counseling is needed, referrals will be made. This does not mean that

the elder will not be an active listener. But this listening role is limited in both duration and scope. The elder listens for the sake of prayer. More, the initial meeting is not the only time the elder will pray about this concern. *Importance of community.* While this part of the conversation begins with assurances of confidentiality, some effort should be made to encourage the widening of the prayer circle. The elder might ask, "Are there two or three others who might help both of us as we share this burden?" or, "Can I share this with the elder group? We guard confidences strictly as a group, and these are my trusted partners. I think you could trust them too." *Duration.* At East County we cautioned strongly against open-ended pastoral commitments. For both ministry staff and elders we encouraged no more than three meetings. Beyond three meetings, ongoing care needed to be renegotiated and others brought into the circle. "Let's agree," the elder might say, "to meet twice more for prayer. If this situation still demands our attention we need to invite others to join us. This is good not only for you, but for me as well."

One final word here. Obviously, great care needs to be given in situations where elders are providing care for women. Many churches require two persons to be present in these situations, or that they occur in public places, or both. At East County, the church helped us identify trusted women who received the same training in pastoral prayer as our elders. These women were publicly acknowledged before the church and in special services received people for prayer.

PRAYERS FOR SPECIFIC CONCERNS

In addition to developing a pre-prayer interview, the elders at East County prepared for the ministry of prayer by anticipating various contexts in which they might be called upon to provide care. Illness, confession of sin, conflict with others, and complaint against God were a few of the situations we envisioned as occasions for prayer. What would it mean to pray for people in those situations? Were there resources we could call upon to help us pray effectively in light of specific circumstances? These questions provided the occasion for developing prayer templates. These templates attempted to bring theological reflection to the task of praying in specific situations. They were not developed as rigid constructs. Clearly, in prayer there is a certain openness that allows for speaking and also listening. Still, these templates gave us useful frameworks that helped shape prayerful imagination.

While we learned from Paul and the ministry of Jesus the nature of pastoral care, we took many of our cues on prayer from the Psalms. Patrick Miller's book, *They Cried to the Lord*, was especially useful. We also read Richard Foster's book, *Prayer: Finding the Heart's True Home*. Our discussions concerning prayer were rich and engaging, and pushed us all deeper into prayer in our personal lives as well.

The intentionality brought to specific pastoral contexts was particularly helpful regarding prayers for healing and complaint. We weren't certain how we felt about our role in praying for healing, or how appropriate it was to bring complaints before God. In both of these areas, we discovered profound resources for ministry.

The elders at East County embraced James 5:13-16 as part of their vocation as elders. Church members responded positively and earnest prayers for healing worked renewal through the church as a whole. We learned a lot through the practice of prayer and anointing with oil. Many of our initial reservations were overcome through actual practice. Some people received dramatic healing, while others experienced no change in their immediate circumstances. All, however, were blessed through the experience.

Our members found prayers of complaint a more challenging prospect. Still, as this practice grew in our church's life, a more robust view of God developed and lives were transformed. What follows is the template the East County elders used to lead people into God's presence through complaint.

Prayer of Complaint

1. *Address.* The address in a prayer of complaint is often stated in very personal terms, "My God, my God..." (Ps 22:2). Such an address is an appeal to relationship. Only within the context of relationship, especially a covenant relationship, can complaint be voiced and heard. Often the personal address is mixed with an attribute of God, which will form the basis of the appeal. God is "my refuge, fortress, stronghold, deliverer, shield, salvation, etc." Such an address, according to Patrick Miller, reflects four foundational beliefs.

1) God's power and willingness to help
2) God's inclination to vindicate the righteous
3) God's guarding and protecting role in times of trouble
4) God's faithfulness which will not leave me abandoned[4]

These beliefs may be important to reiterate before leading someone in a prayer of complaint.

2. *Lament Over Distress.* God is big enough to hear our complaints. It does not threaten our relationship with God to voice our complaints openly and honestly. In fact, such an act reveals faith in God, faith that God can act and make a difference. Dialogue with God is always preferred to silence. But many may hesitate to voice their complaint. Complaining before God may seem irreverent or too personally threatening. Still, voicing complaint is important and may very well open doors

for healing. However, if this is not possible, the elder should voice the complaint on behalf of the sufferer in bold and frank language.

Often the lament portion of a psalm finds expression in a series of questions. For example, "Why are you so far from helping me, from the words of my groaning?" "Why have you forsaken me?" "Why have you cast me off?" It might be good to prepare the complaint before prayer by asking the member to articulate the questions he or she might ask if they could sit across a cup of coffee from God. "If God were here, what questions might you have for him?"

3. *Petition.* One of the hallmarks of the teaching of Jesus on prayer is his insistence on persistence in offering petitions. "Seek, ask, knock," "at least because of persistence he will give whatever he needs," "If you who are evil know how to give good gifts to your children, how much more will your heavenly father give..." (Matt 7:7-11, Luke 11:1-13). This part of the prayer should be bold and direct. Again, elders may encourage petitioners to speak their own requests as the prayer is offered. Even if the petitioner is unable to voice specific concerns, the elder can offer kingdom requests on behalf of the petitioner. By kingdom requests I mean things clearly within the will of God: security, peace, joy, insight, presence, forgiveness, health, etc. These may be things the petitioner feels unworthy to request.

4. *Motivation.* This may be the most important aspect of a prayer of complaint. Why should this prayer be heard by God? Miller suggests that "the character of prayer in Scripture harbors a powerful suggestion that the one who prays can truly engage the deity, can urge reasons upon God for acting in behalf of the one in need, just as God, in giving the law, urges reasons upon

the people for responding and obeying....The mind and heart of God are vulnerable to the pleas *and the arguments* of human creatures."[5] Miller notes three motivations in prayers of complaint in the Old Testament:

1) The righteousness of the petitioner. God should answer the prayer of complaint due to the commitment/behavior of the petitioner. This is often a difficult stance to maintain due to our lack of righteousness. In Christ, however, this motivation becomes more prominent. We make requests boldly because we stand in the righteousness of Christ. Petitions at this point should be made specifically in the name of Jesus. "By the power of Jesus' name we ask..."

2) The nature of God. God's heart and will are sometimes changed in Old Testament narratives by an appeal to God's reputation. For example, Psalm 79 petitions "Help us, O God of our salvation, for the glory of your name, deliver us and forgive our sins, for your name's sake....Why should the nations say, 'Where is their God?'" (See also Ex 34; Num 14:14-17; Dt 9:28; 2 Sam 7:26; 1 Kgs 18:37). If the request of the petitioner can be made in relation to the nature of God, a powerful prayer of faith can emerge. "God, we know that you are the one who saves the downtrodden, who remembers the lowly; we ask that you look now upon Joe and act according to your name."

3) The helplessness of the petitioner. Appeal to God is often made because the petitioner is helpless in accomplishing the desired outcome. God is the only one who can help in this time of need or crisis.

5. *Expression of Confidence or Trust.* The reason we bring this prayer is because we trust God. Ultimately, our

hope is not in the result of the prayer but in God. Therefore, we express our willingness to trust God's timing, care, and provision. For example, Psalm 31:14-15a, "But I trust in you, O Lord; I say 'You are my God.' My times are in your hand. But I trusted in your steadfast love." Notice that the address, motivation, and trust aspects of the prayer correspond very closely to one another.

6. *Vow of Praise*. Sometimes prayers of complaint end with a vow of praise. The vow is not explicitly conditioned upon the specific activity of God, but neither is it made apart from the petition. The logic flows more as follows: "Since God is faithful to act in accordance with his blessed name, I vow to extend my life as praise to him." An example of the vow at the conclusion of prayer is found in Ps. 17:7, "I will give to the Lord the thanks due to his righteousness, and sing praise to the name of the Lord, the Most High."

With this template in mind, imagine composing a prayer to minister to someone whom you know is struggling with complaint before God. How will you lead in the prayer? How will he or she participate? How will you model a way of prayer that the person can continue on her own? How will you make sure that God is the prime actor in this scene? You may wish to write your prayer out in detail.

CONCLUSION

Elders may be known for many things. They might be perceived as visionaries, leading God's flock into the future. Or they might be perceived as guardians, keeping the flock of God from danger. Or as teachers, feeding the people of God with nourishing doctrine. These tasks are all important. My experience with the East County elders suggests that leaders known for their commitment to prayer inspire great confidence in church members. By pointing beyond themselves to God through the practice of prayer, elders help create an environment through which the healing presence of the Spirit becomes vivid and sustaining.

Notes

1. Fred Craddock, *Philippians* (Atlanta, GA: John Knox, 1985), 6.

2. Henri Nouwen, *The Living Reminder: Service and Prayer in Memory of Jesus Christ* (New York: Seabury, 1977), 45, 47.

3. I worked for eleven years as Minister of the Word for the East County Church of Christ in Gresham, Oregon. One of the great privileges I experienced was working with elders devoted to the ministry of prayer. For Dan, Rodger, Keith, Lonnie, Bob, Gary, Peter, John, Bruce and Merrell I give thanks. Most of what follows came from my work with these devoted shepherds.

4. Patrick Miller, *They Cried to the Lord: The Form and Theology of Biblical Prayer* (Minneapolis, MN: Fortress, 1994), 57-58.

5. Miller, 114.

Bibliography

Bonhoeffer, Dietrich. *Life Together.* New York: Harper & Row, 1954. Bonhoeffer's classic statement on Christian community includes great insight about Christian relationships. He urges that all Christian relationships be mediated in and by Christ and warns of the dangers when the strong members of a community act upon weaker members.

Foster, Richard. P*rayer: Finding the Heart's True Home.* Harper Collins, 1992. Foster's book provides the guidance of one with great experience in various aspects of an active prayer life. It sustained several weeks of great discussion for my work with the East County elders. Foster views prayer through the contemplative tradition with all of its strengths and weaknesses. One glaring omission is the lack of any discussion of the Lord's Prayer.

Miller, Patrick. *They Cried to the Lord: The Form and Theology of Biblical Prayer.* Philadelphia, PA: Fortress, 1994. Miller provides both an insightful and readable treatment on prayer in the Bible. Being an Old Testament scholar, Miller focuses the bulk of his attention on the Psalms as a resource for understanding the nature of prayer. One might wish for greater treatment of prayer in the New Testament. Still, Miller's book is full of both theological and pastoral insight.

Nouwen, Henri. *The Living Reminder: Service and Prayer in the Name of Jesus.* New York: Seabury, 1977. Nouwen's little book is a great primer for pastoral leadership. As the title indicates, Nouwen views the minister as a living reminder of Jesus. As living reminders, leaders heal, guide, and sustain. In each of these aspects of leadership, prayer is essential.

Chapter 3

Soul Care and
the Heart of a Shepherd

David Wray

My first elders' meeting remains vivid in my mind. Eight men from sixty to eighty years of age gathered around a highly polished conference table to discuss the affairs of the church. Just one week into my new ministry position, I found myself in a major conflict between the youth deacons and elders over "mixed swimming." Plans for a beach party and a Saturday of surf and sun had excited the youth and their sponsors. Less than ten minutes into this initial meeting, I transformed from a novice to a full participant in church conflict when one elder said, "We want you to stop this nonsense of mixed bathing at the beach. The youth sponsors don't listen to us, so we commission you to convince them that this is a sinful activity."

Arguing that I was only six days on the job fell on deaf ears, so I scheduled a meeting with the youth deacons. With quarrelsome voices youth sponsors caricatured the elders as stubborn and out of touch. One spokesperson said, "They avoid teenagers like the plague. They don't even know where our youth classes meet." He continued his tirade: "When they meet as elders they spend all of their time on administration and management. I pray for the day when our elders show more love for people than for running the church. Is that asking too much?"

A compromise between the elders and deacons required the teenagers to wear "cover-ups" over their swimming suits. When the beach day arrived not one young person wore a tee shirt during a morning of swimming. When sunburn became a problem after lunch they covered up for protection. Then the six elders made a surprise mid-afternoon visit to the beach. They had driven more than an hour to police the situation. Upon arrival they looked around, saw everyone wearing a covering, got back in their car satisfied and drove home. Fourteen months later the Lord called me to graduate school.

Leadership in congregations today is much different than 1967 when I ventured into its deep waters. In that era "trustees" or "boards of directors" often defined the role and responsibilities of elders. Working like a board of directors, elders managed congregational affairs. They supervised staff, controlled budgets, maintained facilities, coordinated ministers, and planned missions. In some cases they served as congregational "policemen" insuring that everyone obeyed all the rules. Often utilizing business models framed a half-century before, the church selected elders based on organizational and supervisory skills. Thus congregations were well organized, but relationships, shepherding, and soul care received little attention. Over emphasizing the "overseer's" role as supervisor, churches often failed to select leaders gifted in shepherding.

Later in my ministry career, we found ourselves in another city, a different church, and with a new staff. The meta-narrative of the new congregation was shepherding God's people. During my seventeen-year staff tenure I learned much about the heart of a shepherd. When I resigned that ministry role to become a university professor, my letter of resignation contained words reflecting on the impact of those elders.

Much of what I have done as a minister I learned from being with you through the years. Your servant-hearts guided an inexperienced young man into a minister who loves using his spiritual gifts to minister to others. Thank you for all you taught me in word and deed.

Much of what I did as a father through those years was because I carefully watched many of you parent. Not only did you parent your own children, but as spiritual parents of this church family, you gave your lives to helping many of us become more like Jesus Christ. Thank you for the ways you spiritually formed me as a parent.

Much of what I know and practice in my prayer life I gleaned from you. An individual could not help but be powerfully impacted by praying with such godly men week after week. Thank you for being prayerful shepherds. Thank you for teaching me to treasure prayer, to pray without ceasing, and to allow the Spirit to take my prayer groanings and utterances and make them known to the Father.

Much of what I do in relating to people I saw demonstrated by you. "Coming down on the side of compassion" forms a core component in my rule of life. I learned that rule from watching and participating many times with you as you gently dealt with difficult circumstances. It did not matter what the issue, I cannot remember a time during the last seventeen years when you acted in a capricious or uncompassionate manner. Thank you for providing me with principles that govern every interaction I have with people.

Spiritual growth, shepherding, and Christ-likeness were refreshing biblical principles evident in this congregation. They formed me as a man of God and gave definition to shepherding

God's people.[1] Godly living, biblical sermons and classes called people to God. Rather than concentrating on congregational policing, leaders modeled an image of Jesus Christ. Elder gatherings provided opportunities for disciples to come for prayer, affirmation, and encouragement. Shepherding nurtured the members, called everyone to holy living, and pastored staff members and their families. Shepherds sought to "smell like sheep,"[2] and men stepped out of the boardroom into the pasture.

Both testaments provide a fertile metaphor for shepherding. Matthew describes God's compassionate heart for sheep wandering without a shepherd. John shows Jesus as the quintessential shepherd. Paul exhorts shepherds to watch over and guard the flock. No one reading the narrative in Acts visualizes a board of directors surrounding Paul as they embraced and prayed. In addition to the Gospels and Pauline literature, the epistles of Peter charge elders to shepherd like Jesus (I Pet. 5:1-5). Elders cannot escape the biblical conceptions of pastoral leaders. They must be with and know people: their needs, concerns, and problems. Shep-herds' lives and hearts welcome and receive every member of their flock. They must be available! Effective shepherds prayerfully develop a congregational culture that permits and expects godly men to involve themselves in pastoring.[3]

The Old Testament provides bountiful shepherding concepts. "The Lord is my shepherd," the psalmist declares, and proceeds to mine the wealth of wisdom which characterizes the conscientious shepherd. Jeremiah 50:6 and Isaiah 40:11 both witness to the importance of shepherding. While it is true that the word "shepherd" in biblical times referred to the kings of Israel, implications drawn from the metaphor serve today's elders well.

Congregational leaders find richness in exploring Ezekiel 34 as a reminder of the high and holy calling of shepherds. Ezekiel draws sharp contrasts between God's shepherding and our feeble attempts as under-shepherds. God expects under-shepherds to have his unconditional love for sheep.[4] Labeling Ezekiel 34:4

as "spirit description," rather than "job description," my para-
phrase reads, "You have strengthened the weak, healed the sick,
and bound up the injured. You have brought back the strays,
searched for the lost. You have ruled them kindly and gently."
Each of these qualities frames the responsibilities of shepherds in
the twenty-first century, and provides us a biblical shepherding
model. Tasks given in this passage concentrate on relationships
and challenge us to live near the sheep.

In what follows I discuss five spiritual qualities for shepherds
who provide care for their flocks. Relational, pastoral, and ministerial skills are seminal throughout this "spirit description." I
explore: 1) effective ways to identify and support weak disciples;
2) how to participate in God's healing process for sick and
injured Christians; 3) ways to search for brothers and sisters who
go astray; 4) effective strategies for reaching the lost; and 5) the
necessity of ministering with kindness and gentleness. Shepherds
embodying this "spirit description" are co-laborers with God in
leading flocks toward spiritual maturity and abundant life.

STRENGTHEN THE WEAK

Because shepherds know the sheep, they are able to identify
and strengthen the weak. Time consuming administrative and
managerial responsibilities make it difficult to know everyone's
needs and to identify struggling Christians. Since "everybody's
business is nobody's business," it is important to place members
into shepherding groups. These groups, ideally twenty or fewer
families, make it possible for shepherds to identify and care for
vulnerable disciples. Lynn Anderson invites elders to consider,
"What are we, if we don't have a flock?"[5] We may be organized,
active in good deeds, efficient and effective administrators, but
without a flock an elder is not a shepherd.

In our frenetic world elders often wonder how to find adequate time for pastoring, disciplining, and maturing the spiritually
weak. Such demands cause few people to rush to volunteer.

Godly shepherding demands that leaders seek first God's right-eousness and, as servants of Jesus, live sacrificially. In contrast, elderships built like the board of trustees will create plenty of volunteers.[6]

As elders transition to shepherds they learn to spiritually *form* as well as *inform* their flock. Using the metaphor of child-birth, Paul desired that Christ be *formed* in the Galatians (4:19). This is the biblical mandate for our shepherding. Our goal, like Paul's, is that Christlikeness be formed in every disciple. God, of course, is the one who forms disciples into the image of his son, Jesus Christ. But shepherds are co-laborers with Him in the process. We serve as God's co-laborers by equipping, nurturing, and walking alongside others. Our co-laboring opportunities establish us as spiritual exemplars and mentors. Like the apostle Paul, we invite our flock to imitate us as we imitate Jesus.

Rather than doing all of the work of ministry, wise shepherds invite maturing brothers and sisters to participate with them. Ephesians 4:11-16, a practical theology of ministry, claims that spiritually gifted leaders equip people for the work of ministry. The result: the body of Christ is built up and works of service abound. Leaders sometimes find it easier to perform ministry alone, which means that other disciples miss the benefit of per-sonally observing and practicing their spiritual gifts. Cleaning a child's room may be easier than teaching the child to clean his/her own room but will cripple the child's developing respon-sibility. Wise parents invite children to participate in the cleaning, equipping them for a lifetime of responsible behavior. In the same way, growing brothers and sisters mature by observing experienced shepherds minister and practice spiritual disciplines. Inviting others to join us in ministry experiences pays enormous dividends when our co-pastoring brothers and sisters perform ordinary acts of helpfulness, becoming "strong" in the Lord.[7]

"Spiritual *formation*" acknowledges that spiritual growth often includes "transforming moments." After returning from Asia,

Paul states that he and his companions experienced immense pressure, far beyond their ability to endure, despairing of life, even feeling the gloom of a death sentence (2 Cor. 1:8-9). Every day in our congregations, members share Paul's despair and hopelessness. The death of a loved one, a significant loss, a lingering illness, or a catastrophic event pushes our people to anguish. At these times of spiritual struggle shepherds who are near may be ready to join God in the reconciliation process.

Elders in some congregations are discovering that their weekly meetings provide ideal contexts in which to shepherd. When shepherds come together to spiritually strengthen the weak, to pray with those who are struggling, and to help form disciples into the image of Christ, there is much to celebrate. These types of gatherings stand in stark contrast to traditional elders meetings which spend the preponderance of time on governance.

HEAL THE SICK

Not only are shepherds passionate about strengthening the weak, we also respond to our calling of unconditionally loving and caring for the sick. Sickness may manifest itself physically, mentally, or spiritually.

God, our great physician, daily cares for all kinds of sickness. Psalm 103:2-3 says: "Bless the Lord, O my soul, and do not forget all his benefits—who forgives all your iniquity, who heals all your diseases." Because there is a special place in God's heart for the sick, our hearts beat with his in compassionately caring for the ill.

Sick sheep are vulnerable. Medication and bandages are essential tools to help shepherds care for defenseless sheep. Health care providers supply physical "medication and bandages," but shepherds create opportunities to encourage suffering disciples when they transition from meeting around a conference table to a living room and designate specific times for members to pray with shepherds.

I dream of a day when members first think to call shepherds in times of physical, emotional, and spiritual sickness. Shepherds then respond with prayers and anointing with oil. Prayer and anointing by elders, as admonished in James, creates healthy faith communities. "Is any one of you sick? He should call the elders of the church to pray over him and anoint him with oil in the name of the Lord. And the prayer offered in faith will make the sick person well; the Lord will raise him up" (James 5:14-15).

Recently I visited the hospital room of a terminally ill woman. Two other shepherds joined me in response to her request for prayer and anointing with oil. Fear came into her eyes as she talked about impending death. I could sense her dread when she said, "I haven't done enough good deeds. I haven't really loved the lost because if I had, I would have taught more people about Christ." Our prayer and anointing conveyed God's peace and presence. When I saw her several days later she stunned me by her pronouncement of healing. Knowing she was in hospice care, I asked her what medical breakthrough occurred. "Oh," she said, "nothing has changed in my medical condition. I have been healed of the guilt and the fear of dying. Thank you for anointing me with oil so I could experience God's healing." God heals in many ways.

In addition to prayer and anointing with oil, the practice of "laying on of hands," described in Acts 6:6 and Acts 13:3, provides disciples with peace. When elders gather around those new to a congregation, or the sick, or to affirm people's use of their spiritual gifts, something sacred happens. Prayer transforms the disciple's spirit and meaningful touch conveys grace and peace.

BIND UP THE INJURED

An interesting phenomenon occurs when the elders' central concern is to bind up the injured. They often begin providing spiritual care during times of grief and loss. Since shepherds closely identify with their people, they visit hospitals, conduct funerals, and participate in other pastoral ministries usually delegated to church staff. Bereaved Christians need words of comfort, especially from their shepherds. These intimate "holy ground" times unite sheep with their shepherd.

Not only do funerals and times of crisis create sacred time with sheep in one's flock, they may also be the times when Satan bruises people with stones from his evil arsenal. Shepherds living during Ezekiel's time knew the danger of wild animals roaming the countryside looking for injured prey. Just as sheep suffer wounds and broken limbs from the dangers of the pasture, Christians today can easily become "cast." Cast is a word all shepherds understand. Because the wool of sheep is heavy and bulky, sometimes wounded sheep stumble and cannot get up. Shepherds have only a matter of hours to get a cast sheep back on its feet. If that does not happen, the sheep dies. All shepherds are vigilant for cast sheep. Elders must also be attentive in watching for cast sheep in their flock. When we do not help one of our injured brothers or sisters get upright when they are down, they likely will die.

How many times are elders the last to know when a member is cast because of separation or divorce? Why are we unaware of serious conflict among members in our congregation until division is already a reality? How often are we in the dark about a child who is acting out in the family, causing untold grief and pain? When we take seriously the binding up of the injured, the earliest call disciples make is to the shepherd of their soul. When we are busy making decisions about carpet in the building, leaky roofs, and how contributions are distributed, wounded "cast" sheep lay helplessly on the ground. Our people are desperate for shepherds whose lives overflow with love and tender care. Just as the Chief Shepherd cares for all Christians, God appoints elders to live in the pasture with sheep and constantly attend to broken hearted, despairing, and spiritually cast sheep. Binding up the injured addresses pasture sheep, but what about sheep that have wandered away from the flock?

BRING BACK THE STRAYS

Scripture is replete with descriptions of the ways in which our loving God cares for sheep gone astray. As a tender shepherd, God gathers lambs and carries them close to his heart and gently leads those that have young by their side (Isaiah 40:11, John 10:12-14, I Peter 2:24-25). Satan moves throughout the land seeking lambs to devour. Paul warns elders to be alert for savage attacks. For their protection shepherds daily lead sheep to lush green meadows and quiet waters. When sheep wander from safety, courageous shepherds leave their flocks and go into the wilderness seeking strays.

In today's economy it doesn't make sense to spend too much time on losses. The conventional wisdom, "cut your losses and move on," however, ignores the biblical principle of leaving everything to find the lost sheep. Jesus turns common wisdom upside down, reframing the issue with this stunning suggestion: "Suppose one of you has a hundred sheep and loses one of them. Does he not leave the ninety-nine in the open country and go after the lost sheep until he finds it? And when he finds it, he joyfully puts it on his shoulders and goes home...I tell you that in the same way there will be more rejoicing in heaven over one sinner who repents than over ninety-nine righteous persons who do not need to repent" (John 15:4-7).

Today's elders refuse to rest until each sheep is safe. They know this only happens when we have the smell of sheep on us. Handshakes and casual interaction in the church building do not cause us to smell like our sheep. It occurs only when shepherds are familiar with the needs of their sheep and agonize over their pain. Eating meals together, conversing on the phone, and participating in small groups allow elders to know those who are growing and those in peril. Shepherding groups may provide the most effective means for closely monitoring healthy and stray sheep.

As I sat in his dark living room, blinds drawn shut, a distraught father described the agony of the past five days. His sixteen-year-old daughter decided to run away from home and live on her own. He wept openly trying to articulate his indescribable emptiness and fear. Each passing car caused him to rush to the window, part the blinds, and look out, hoping that his prodigal daughter had returned.

Throughout the conversation, I prayed and reflected on what our churches might be like if shepherds had the same urgent spiritual passion to watch for strays. The distraught father's longing to receive his daughter back demonstrated the heart of God. Great was the celebration when the daughter returned home. Sitting in that living room with him after her return, the sunlight pouring through the windows, the father said repeatedly, "She was lost and now she is found." May God constantly raise up faithful shepherds who run to returning prodigals, embrace returning sheep, and rejoice with homecoming parties.

SEARCH FOR THE LOST

Today when an individual is lost in the wilderness, massive searches occur. Scores of people spread out over the area seeking the missing person. In the same ways biblical leaders seek the lost. Wise shepherds recognize that evangelistic strategies of the past often fail to reach lost people in this new millennium. Evangelism is dormant across North America, with seventy-five percent of American congregations reporting stagnation or decline. This creates weighty questions among shepherds about the gospel and this culture. Christianity in North America is floundering with an identity crisis.

Churches, marginalized in the last fifty years, no longer possess the power and authority they once enjoyed. This marginalization occurred in part because North American churches concentrated on marketing the church and providing "goods and services" to members in good standing.[8] "The vocabulary of commerce and the syntax of consumption not only distorts our relationship with God and thus with each other, they also miscast the church in the role of retail vendor, trading in spiritual goods and services."[9] When congregations discuss *meeting needs* and *customer satisfaction*, they miss God's design for the church. Consumer-oriented leaders might ask new members, "Why did you decide to be members of this church?" often receiving responses indicating personal benefits. "I like the worship," or "The youth ministry is second to none," or "My adult class discusses interesting topics." In contrast, shepherds might instead ask, "In what ways can this faith community help you to mature as a disciple of Jesus?" or "How may we help you live fully into your baptismal commitment?" Customer service provides the best goods and services in town but will produce marginalized and inauthentic churches with little gospel, much religion, and no mission.[10]

More than one hundred million North Americans, constituting one-third of the U.S. population in the 2000 census, now live in multi-housing units. Less than five percent of this population have any church affiliation. These residents now compose the largest "unchurched" group in North America.[11] "Build it and they will come" does not attract this population. Church leaders must "search for the lost" with innovative strategies.[12] The following stories demonstrate strategies that enlist us as participants.

Gary and Maria White requested and received permission to conduct a summer Vacation Bible School on Wednesday nights in the courtyard of an apartment complex. The White's mission team spent the summer months teaching children and youth the good news of Jesus. School days brought an invitation from the apartment manager to continue "church" in an apartment, without cost, throughout the fall and winter. "You have made a real difference in the lives of our residents, and I want you to continue." Seven years later, Christians gathering each week for worship and ministry fill two apartments. The Whites took bold steps to establish a viable strategy for searching for the lost in the twenty-first century.

Joyce Dalzell created FaithWorks "to help the underemployed acquire the confidence and skills for gainful employment through personal, academic, career, and spiritual development."[13] Instruction in life skills, biblical principles, and healthy lifestyles develop productive Christians. Unpaid internships with Christian tutors and mentors prepare students for Christian vocations. Each week more than fifty volunteers minister to FaithWorks students, serving as teachers, mentors, counselors, social workers, and community liaisons. Church leaders, committed to serving people oppressed by poverty, commit time and resources to equipping disciples for ministries like FaithWorks.

Twenty-first century shepherds will live out the gospel in North America by preparing disciples to leave church "fortresses," engage the culture, and participate in the transforming work of God. Instead of bogging down in endless conversations, elders will boldly lead congregations into the twenty-first century seeking lost sheep.

KINDLY AND GENTLY LEAD

Many of the kings of Israel during the period from 900-100 BC treated their subjects indifferently, ruling them with harshness and brutality. Rough treatment, no matter how expressed, destroys relationships. A short time on the farm reveals the harsh and brutal ways animals seek dominance over their own kind. Chickens establish a pecking order. West Texas sheep ranchers report that a powerful "bully sheep" often dominates their flocks. Little peace abides in a flock when a dominant animal makes life miserable for the others. Biblical shepherds in God's kingdom recognize the danger of dominance. Rather than responding in kind with severity, shepherds display Christlikeness by humility of heart (Matt. 11:28-29).

How many gentle men do you know? In writing a tribute to a long-time elder recently, gentleness emerged as his most characteristic trait. Upon further reflection I realized how few gentle men I know. Our culture loudly proclaims the benefit of assertiveness and domination. Popular leadership literature rarely mentions gentleness as a core value, but scripture provides a contrast to society's voice.

Gentle shepherds possess the power of changing wrath to reason. The word *epieikeia* (gentleness) is translated "patience," "softness," "forbearance," "moderation," or "sweet reasonableness." Instead of treating sinners with disdain, shepherds restore gently. Being a gentle person manifests itself in joy, peace, kindness, goodness, faithfulness, gentleness, and self-control (Gal. 5:22-23).

When I speak about kindness and gentleness as essential shepherding qualities, someone inevitably raises a question about elder authority. But does scripture sanction any other authority but moral suasion? The KJV translates I Timothy 3:1, "If a man desires the *office* of a bishop, he desireth a good work." That translation holds elders up as "office holders," empowered with all the rights and privileges thereof. The word *office* implies a conveyed sense of power, influence, and authority. In seventeenth-century England and the Anglican Church, office holding was normative; however early manuscripts, from the second and third centuries, more accurately translate I Timothy 3:1, "If anyone desires to bishop." The word *office* does not appear in early manuscripts and in many other translations commonly used today.[14] The authority of shepherds, prescribed by Scripture, comes from their example and relationships rather than from an official position. Henri Nouwen provides helpful imagery of a non-authoritarian leader:

Here we touch the most important quality of Christian leadership in the future. It is not a leadership of power and control, but a leadership of powerlessness and humility in which the suffering servant of God, Jesus Christ, is made manifest....I am speaking of leadership in which power is constantly abandoned in favor of love. It is a true spiritual leadership. Powerlessness and humility in the spiritual life do not refer to people who have no spine and who let everyone else make decisions for them. They refer to people who are so deeply in love with Jesus that they are ready to follow him wherever he guides them, always trusting that, with him, they will find life and find it abundantly.[15]

Both Scripture and contemporary literature urge shepherds to avoid controlling and ruthless leadership practices. Jesus condemned the practice of lording it over others. When "Mrs. Zebedee" came to Jesus requesting that her two sons become his most prominent disciples, Jesus was appalled. His response proved disquieting: "Whoever wants to become great among you must be your servant, and whoever wants to be first must be your slave—just as the Son of Man did not come to be served, but to serve, and to give his life as a ransom for many" (Matt. 20:22-25). Approachable gentle men receive respect and honor from the flock. These servants willingly lay down their lives for the sheep, and they constantly practice the ways of the Chief Shepherd.

CONCLUSION

Shepherding in twenty-first century North America challenges leaders regardless of the number of years served. At a recent ElderLink one elder observed, "I have been an *elder* in the Lord's church for twenty years, but I have only been a *shepherd* for the past five years. I regret becoming a shepherd so late in life." Delegating administrative matters allows shepherds time for God's people. Ezekiel's "spirit description" provides a spiritual compass for shepherds in today's churches.

As we engage in the blessing of shepherding, strengthening the weak, healing the sick, binding up the injured, and seeking the lost, lives change and disciples mature. Our attitudes and actions reflect Christlikeness in our compassionate care of flocks.

Realizing that the new millennium is changing swiftly and dramatically, we commit ourselves to learning new ministry strategies and engaging in bold and courageous new evangelism approaches, which equip disciples for full missional engagement in homes, work environments, and places of recreation. With the Chief Shepherd leading us through the power of his Holy Spirit, we rejoice daily in living out the principles and practices of Ezekiel 34.

NOTES

1. Henri Nouwen, in *In the Name of Jesus: Reflections on Christian Leadership* (New York: Crossroad, 1989), looks back on a life of teaching at several Ivy League schools, and his ministry in a mentally handicapped community. Nouwen reflects on the challenges and biblical principles for today's Christian leaders seeking to live the Christlife. He notes that leaders should avoid asking: How many people take you seriously? How much are you going to accomplish? Can you show some results? Rather, leaders should be questioning, Are you in love with Jesus? Do you know the incarnate God? Nouwen declares, "In our world of loneliness and despair, there is an enormous need for men and women who know the heart of God, a heart that forgives, that cares, that reaches out and wants to heal. In that heart there is no suspicion, no vindictiveness, no resentment, and not a tinge of hatred. It is a heart that suffers immensely because it sees the magnitude of human pain and the great resistance to trusting God who wants to offer consolation and hope" (24). Two of Nouwen's thirty books specifically address the character and virtues of spiritual leaders. In *The Wounded Healer* (Garden City, NY: Image Books, 1979), Nouwen suggests that ministry is about "one beggar sharing bread with another hungry beggar." *The Way of the Heart* (New York: Ballentine Books,

1981), encourages readers to constantly practice solitude, silence, and prayer as a path to Christlikeness.

2. See Lynn Anderson, *They Smell Like Sheep: Spiritual Leadership for the 21st Century* (West Monroe, LA: Howard Publishing, 1997).

3. Exploring numerous biblical examples, Gene A. Getz, in *Elders and Leaders: God's Plan for Leading the Church* (Chicago: Moody, 2003), suggests that Ezekiel 34 and Acts 20 provide ideal models for elders today.

4. Each time the Highland Church of Christ in Abilene, TX, adds new shepherds, John Willis, professor of Old Testament at Abilene Christian University, presents a lesson from Ezekiel 34:4. Willis observes that Ezekiel 34 provides the most comprehensive description of God's work among us as a "shepherd."

5. Anderson argues, at his National Shepherding Clinics, that church members automatically develop close relationships with elders when the leaders are true shepherds. One can serve a congregation as a trustee and develop few pastoral relationships with members; however, a good number of congregations today are designating "shepherding groups," seeking to provide spiritual care for every member of the flock.

6. Alexander Strauch, *Biblical Eldership: An Urgent Call to Restore Biblical Church Leadership* (Littleton, CO: Lewis & Roth Publishers, 1997).

7. Jack Cummins asks about who is ultimately responsible for the care of these weak disciples of Jesus. He concludes that when God turns to ask who will make such disciples stronger, it is the shepherds. See *Leaven* 2 (Winter Quarter 1992).

8. For a theological framework for missional ecclesiology, see Darrell L. Guder, editor, *Missional Church: A Vision for the Sending of the Church in North America* (Grand Rapids, MI: Eerdmans, 1998). Rather than congregations being venders of goods and services, the writers recommend reclaiming the priesthood of all believers to be "ministers" and "missionaries," not just those who serve as ministerial staff. Perhaps the best practical treatment of the missional church is Lois Y. Barrett, et al., *Treasure in Clay Jars: Patterns in Missional Faithfulness* (Grand Rapids, MI:. Eerdmans, 2004). Eight patterns of missional church are examined in nine or ten congregations in North America. For additional resources see the Gospel and Our Culture website: www. gocn.org.

9. *StormFront: The Good News of God* (Grand Rapids, MI: Eerdmans, 2003). Written by four authors with an understanding of the

Gospel and our culture, the book asks how the Gospel is heard in a twenty-first-century post-modern culture.

10. Alan J. Roxburgh, writing in *The Missionary Congregation, Leadership and Liminality* (Harrisburg, PA: Trinity Press International, 1997), outlines ways in which North American congregations are being marginalized in today's culture. He describes leadership characteristics required to lead missionary congregations in North America. Rather than church leaders returning to the "good old days," and to a mythical time when Christianity enjoyed strength and supremacy, Roxburgh challenges shepherds to boldly come into God's future, embracing God's call to this generation.

11. See Stetzer, ed., *Planting New Churches in a Postmodern Age* (Nashville, TN: Broadman & Holman, 2003).

12. For significant biblical and theological strategies connecting the twenty-first-century church with the first-century church, see Roger Gehring, *Home Church and Mission: The Importance of Household Structures in Early Christianity* (Peabody, MA: Hendrickson, 2004).

13. Modeled after HopeWorks of Memphis and Central Dallas Ministries, FaithWorks of Abilene graduates become employable and grow spiritually. Most enter the program with little or no spiritual background, but after completing thirteen weeks of training, the majority become Christians.

14. Anderson explores "authority," "rule," "bishop," and other important words associated with elders in the KJV Bible in *They Smell Like Sheep*, chapter 13. In "Authority and Leadership in the New Testament," *Leaven* 2 (First Quarter, 1992), James W. Thompson provides a study of the New Testament word for "authority." Larry Richards, in *A Theology of Church Leadership* (Grand Rapids, MI: Zondervan, 1980), claims that local leaders in New Testament churches had the primary purpose of leading by example and not the authority to make decisions. Ian Fair, writing in *Leadership in the Kingdom* (Abilene, TX: ACU Press, 1996), provides studies on numerous words concerning the authority of elders.

15. *In the Name of Jesus* (New York: Crossroad, 1989). This volume on leadership stresses spirituality and spiritual formation. His book, *The Return of the Prodigal Son* (New York: Doubleday, 1992), provides seminal principles on ways spiritual leaders should gently and kindly restore God's people.

BIBLIOGRAPHY

Anderson, Lynn. *They Smell Like Sheep*. West Monroe, LA: Howard Publishing, 1997. This volume culminates more than thirty years of research, teaching, and preaching on leadership for the church. Elders seeking to transition from trustees to shepherds find this book a goldmine of helpful principles and practices.

Barrett, Lois Y. et. al. *Treasure in Clay Jars*. Grand Rapids, MI: Eerdmans, 2004. North America is a vast mission field. The Gospel and Our Culture Network suggests that many congregations in North America have reached a plateau or are declining. Barrett and her colleagues examine numerous congregations in North America that are missional, and identify the principles evident in these congregations.

Boa, Kenneth. *Conformed to His Image: Biblical and Practical Approaches to Spiritual Formation*. Grand Rapids, MI: Zondervan, 2001. In our complex world, there is a growing desire among disciples of Jesus for an authentic spirituality that will touch our lives in a meaningful and practical way. Twelve facets or principles for spiritual formation provide an integrated path to the Christlife.

Carson, D. A. *Becoming Conversant With the Emerging Church*. Grand Rapids, MI: Zondervan, 2005. A New Testament professor at Trinity Evangelical Divinity School in Chicago, Carson provides insights and recommendations for the Emerging Church movement of the 21st century. As a biblical scholar, he assists the reader in distinguishing biblical practices and cultural norms.

Fair, Ian A. *Leadership in the Kingdom*. Abilene, TX: ACU Press, 1996. Fair, a New Testament scholar and former Dean of the College of Biblical Studies at Abilene Christian University, presents a biblical servant-leadership model for spiritual leaders. Chapter 12, a word study on various leadership roles in the first century, is worth the price of the book.

Guder, Darrell L., Editor. *Missional Church: A Vision for the Sending of the Church in North America*. Grand Rapids, MI: Eerdmans, 1998. Providing a theology of the church, this volume claims that North America is now a mission field. Six missiologists challenge the church to recover its missional call in North America. Both theology and a program to equip local churches provide the heart of this book.

Getz, Gene. *Elders and Leaders: God's Plan for Leading the Church.* Chicago: Moody, 2003. Exploring a wide range of topics, Getz, a biblical scholar and author of more than 50 books, returns repeatedly to Scripture in establishing biblical and cultural principles for leaders in today's churches.

Nouwen, Henri. *In the Name of Jesus.* New York: Crossroad, 1989. Working primarily from Matthew 4:1-11, the narrative surrounding the circumstances of Satan's three temptations of Jesus, Nouwen provides fresh insights about how spiritual leaders must fight against the temptations to be relevant, to exert personal influence, and to use power inappropriately. The pregnant concepts in this book demand rereading several times each year.

Nouwen, Henri. *The Way of the Heart.* New York: Ballantine Books, 1981. Calling spiritual leaders to solitude, silence, and prayer, this volume reminds us of our solidarity in brokenness with all of humanity, and encourages us to reach out to anyone in need. In these three spiritual practices, we enter into the heart of God, and we become more aware of God's active presence in our lives and the lives of those we lead.

Roxburgh, Alan J. *The Missionary Church, Leadership, and Liminality.* Harrisburgh, PA: Trinity Press International, 1997. An extensive series, "Christian Mission and Modern Culture," includes this volume as one of the offerings. "Liminality" simply means that we can only go forward, never backwards. While some church leaders want to return to the "good old days of yester year," Roxburgh argues that while the future is unknown, God is already in the future preparing the way for disciples around the world.

Willard, Dallas. *Renovation of the Heart.* Colorado Springs, CO: NavPress, 2002. Few authors provide insights for spiritual formation as well as Dallas Willard. This volume is about general patterns of personal transformation, not formulas and programmatic strategies. After reading this work, you will have a better grasp of what it means to be a disciple of Jesus who is growing more into his likeness every day.

Chapter 4

I WAS SICK, AND
YOU LOOKED AFTER ME

Pastoral Leadership in Ministering to the Sick

Rubel Shelly

Mark and Melanie were having their best year ever in 1999. They had met on a "blind date" four years earlier, fallen in love, and married. Gracie was born in March 1999, and only a few weeks after that Mark, Melanie, and Gracie moved into their new house.

There was so much joy. So many things to celebrate. So many things for which God's name was blessed in that house! For Mark and Melanie believed with all their hearts that every good thing in their lives—in all of creation, in fact—begins in the loving, overflowing heart of God! But Mark was also getting sick in that same year—unaware of the sinister disease that was taking control of his body even as all those beautiful times were being shared.

Mark noticed that his knee was swelling and giving him pain. So there was a visit to his physician. An x-ray and MRI and blood work were ordered. The intruder was unmasked on a Friday in December. Mark was told he had leukemia. The medications started that very day. And so did the decision-making about whether God's name would continue to be blessed in the Burress family.

After stopping at the pharmacy to fill the first of the countless prescriptions, Mark pulled into his driveway. He had formed a plan—a gentle plan—for telling Melanie about the diagnosis that still had his head reeling. But all that went by the boards as they met, and Mark simply blurted out, "I have cancer." The two of them held each other and cried. Then they went to see their beautiful baby through their tears. They talked that night. And prayed. And wondered what they would do with their awful news. *Was Jesus there that afternoon?*

JESUS: DIVINE COMPASSION ON DISPLAY

When we read the Gospels, there are all those encounters with hurt and sick people and his compassionate reaction to their sad plight. So we read how he healed a paralyzed man whose friends lowered him through a ripped-open roof (Mark 2:1-12).[1] On the way to respond to Jairus's desperate plea for his daughter (Mark 9:21-24a), Jesus healed a woman whose constant hemorrhages over twelve years had not only put her through painful medical treatments but had emptied her purse (Mark 24b-34). He healed a man who had been blind from birth—in the unsympathetic context of a theological debate about the causes of human suffering! (John 9:1-12). While the list of Jesus' sympathetic acts toward suffering persons is long, the case of the man blind from birth is particularly instructive:

> Walking down the street, Jesus saw a man blind from birth. His disciples asked, "Rabbi, who sinned: this man or his parents, causing him to be born blind?"
>
> Jesus said, "You're asking the wrong question. You're looking for someone to blame. There is no such cause–effect here. Look instead for what God can do. We need to be energetically at work for the One who

sent me here, working while the sun shines. When night falls, the workday is over. For as long as I am in the world, there is plenty of light. I am the world's Light."

He said this and then spit in the dust, made a clay paste with the saliva, rubbed the paste on the blind man's eyes, and said, "Go, wash at the Pool of Siloam" (Siloam means "Sent"). The man went and washed—and saw.

Soon the town was buzzing. His relatives and those who year after year had seen him as a blind man begging were saying, "Why, isn't this the man we knew, who sat here and begged?"

Others said, "It's him all right!"

But others objected, "It's not the same man at all. It just looks like him."

He said, "It's me, the very one."

They said, "How did your eyes get opened?"

"A man named Jesus made a paste and rubbed it on my eyes and told me, 'Go to Siloam and wash.' I did what he said. When I washed, I saw."

"So where is he?"

"I don't know."[2]

The disciples traveling with Jesus on that particular day apparently held the common-to-their-day view that physical suffering always traces to divine judgment. People go broke "because they deserve it" or get sick "because God is trying to tell them something." That perspective on suffering is still around! So one of the first questions people are conditioned to ask when they get a horrible diagnosis or get hurt in an automobile accident is "What did I do to deserve this?"

DOES HUMAN SUFFERING MERIT OUR COMPASSION?

To be sure, no thinking person would deny that some physical suffering is the result of personal sin. An alcoholic who dies of cirrhosis of the liver, a criminal fleeing the police who flips a car and is paralyzed from a broken neck, an arsonist who is severely burned while setting a blaze—all these reflect situations where somebody has brought a horrible fate on himself.[3]

But it is a mistake to hold that everything bad that happens to a human being happens because she is being punished. The Book of Job is in the Bible to counter such a wrong-headed view of things. Jesus stood against such an interpretation of human tragedy. For example, when told about the deaths of some Galilean Jews at the hands of Pilate, he asked the rhetorical question, "Do you think that these Galileans were worse sinners than all the other Galileans because they suffered this way?" (Luke 13:2). He went further to raise a case his hearers apparently knew about that involved a construction accident: "Or those eighteen who died when the tower in Siloam fell on them—do you think they were more guilty than all the others living in Jerusalem?" (Luke 13:4).

Poverty and wealth are not reliable indicators of character. Neither are sickness and health equivalent to lost and saved or blameworthy and blameless. Cancer and heart disease are no more selective than hurricanes and tornadoes. What of a baby with Down's Syndrome? What of Christians imprisoned in Saudi Arabia or Communist China? What of a four-year-old child kidnapped, raped, and murdered? Can anyone who believes in a God of compassion and love say those things happened as his will? By his choice? At his bidding? If such things are attributed to God in our theologies, how can we expect people to love and trust him? If we believe these horrible things happen to people because God caused them, how could we be justified in feeling compassion for them and trying to relieve their pain?

We've all heard it! "Sweetheart, I'm sorry your baby died. It's just the will of God, and we have to accept it!" Or, "Your cancer is horrible news, but we know that everything happens for a purpose!" *Much of what happens in this world is not God's will,*

and it is a horrible view of God that says otherwise. He does not
will terrorism, murder, lies, and adultery; all these actions are, by
definition, sinful precisely because they are violations of God's
explicit will. Neither does God will the natural tragedies of
earthquakes and tornadoes, plane crashes and car wrecks, birth
defects and blindness. These things happen in a world that
operates under natural law where gravity, metal fatigue in the
wing of a plane, radiation near a just-pregnant woman, and aging
bring about predictable consequences.

But back to John 9 and Jesus' encounter with a blind man
to try to clarify these points. As Jesus and his disciples walked
by him, they asked him, "Rabbi, who sinned, this man or his
parents, that he was born blind?" Their unsympathetic question
reflected the common assumption that people suffer only when
they deserve it. Jesus would have no part in it. He challenged
their leading question with this answer: "Neither this man nor his
parents sinned."

The New International Version, as practically every English
translation of the Gospel of John, makes what I take to be a serious mistake at this point in the text. They punctuate with a
comma to create a longer sentence that reads: "Neither this man
nor his parents sinned, but this happened so that the work of
God might be displayed in his life. As long as it is day, we must
do the work of him who sent me. Night is coming, when no one
can work." The New Revised Standard Version is worse still:
"Neither this man nor his parents sinned; he was born blind so
that God's works might be revealed in him. We must work the
works of him who sent me while it is day; night is coming when
no one can work."

These readings lead one to think that Jesus told his disciples
that God had caused this man to be born without his sight—thus
creating unimaginable heartache for his parents and forcing him
to live with a severe handicap—just so God could put on a healing display during the ministry of Jesus of Nazareth! But can you

really bring yourself to believe a loving, compassionate God would blind a baby for the sake of having a candidate for a miracle two, three, or four decades later? I confess to finding the notion abhorrent! What would you think of a doctor who poured gasoline on someone's leg and lit it so he could demonstrate a remarkable new technique for grafting skin?

The Greek manuscripts from which we make our English translation of the New Testament contain no punctuation. Not even word divisions. So where to supply commas, semi-colons, question marks, periods, and other punctuation marks is a decision for translators. Look at the difference made in the understanding of this passage simply by punctuating it differently. Here are the two verses in question, with a fairly wooden "literal" translation, trying to preserve the word order in the original text. Only the punctuation will be different.

> *Option One:* "Neither this man sinned nor the parents of him, but that might be displayed the works of God in him. It is necessary for us to work the works of the one having sent me while it is day. Night is coming when no one can work."
>
> *Option Two:* "Neither this man sinned nor the parents of him. But that might be displayed the works of God in him, it is necessary for us to work the works of the one having sent me while it is day. Night is coming when no one can work."

I prefer the second translation option: Jesus denies that the man in question is blind because of sin— whether his own or his parents' sin. And he does not say that the poor fellow was made blind by God at his birth so Jesus would have a convenient candidate for miracle-working. On this rendering, Jesus offers no explanation for why the man is blind but does offer to do something to *help* him.

The citation of the fuller text given earlier in this essay is from Eugene Peterson's *The Message*. I like it for the simple reason that it captures what I understand to be going on in this event. Would-be theologians were trying to solve the problem of evil, to account for human suffering in a world created by a loving God. Their thesis was the received wisdom that human pain and misery are typically, if not always, punishment for sin. When they tried their theodicy on the Master Teacher, he told them to quit worrying about academic formulations and to do something for the poor man! Close the distance between their unsympathetic speculation about suffering and find something they could do to make one man's condition better! Stop being so blind themselves! This story is intended to open more eyes than those of the unfortunate man whom Jesus healed that day.

JESUS: OUR MODEL FOR COMPASSION TO SUFFERERS

The work of God in this world is not to blight and blind. It is to help and heal! Neither is his work to explain the unexplainable. It is to show mercy and compassion! So Jesus spit on the ground and made mud with his saliva. Then he took some of the pasty dirt and daubed it over the man's eyelids. He next sent the man to wash off the mud in the waters of the Pool of Siloam. The text says: "So the man went and washed, and came home seeing" (9:7b). Against what you might expect, this powerful deed of compassion didn't turn every heart to Jesus in that town. Some forms of blindness (that is, spiritual hard-heartedness) are more permanent than others.

Here are the preliminary conclusions I want to draw from this episode to guide everything that will follow:

1) Jesus helped this man because he needed help and refused to get into a debate about whether he really deserved it or not.

2) Jesus touched and affirmed a man whose malady

caused many others to keep their distance and to
avoid him.

3) Jesus taught his disciples that their duty is to do what
they can when they can to make the lives of others
better. Opportunities don't last forever.

4) Compassionate deeds to suffering people have no
guaranteed outcome (for example, positive reactions
by recipients or bystanders) and should be performed
simply because they are right.

Because of what the earliest followers of Jesus witnessed in
him, they formed enclaves of love and compassion in the
churches across the Roman Empire. Apostles and evangelists in
those churches taught the earliest believers to "share each
other's troubles and problems" (Gal. 6:2)[4] and commanded that
they "be sympathetic, love as brothers, be compassionate and
humble" (1 Peter 3:8). Pure religion among these first Christians
was not only defined by personal holiness (that is, keeping
themselves unspotted from the world) but also by kind hearts
and helpful actions toward society's most vulnerable members
(James 1:27). With all its failings across the centuries, the church
has never completely lost sight of this obligation to the weak,
helpless, sick and dying.

One of the hallmarks of Christian missionary work in Third
World countries is medical missions. Many of the major hospitals
in large American cities bear the names of Catholic saints (for example, St. Thomas Hospital in Nashville, St. Jude Children's
Research Hospital in Memphis) or Protestant groups (for example, Baptist Hospital, Methodist Hospital, etc.). There is reason
to think that over the next few years to decades, churches and
parachurch groups will play an important role in health care in
the United States as the cost of health care and health insurance
continue to escalate. Who will care for the poor? Who will be
advocates for the most vulnerable? Because so much suffering is

the result of physical and emotional illness, we would naturally expect that ministry to the sick always will be important to the church's witness to a watching world.

Do we really need to prove that one of the most effective ways for a local church to exhibit Christ's presence to its environment is through loving service? Among the most vulnerable and needy are persons whose suffering traces to issues involving their health. Leaders of local churches display their likeness to Christ and make themselves more approachable when they are seen being attentive to such persons and their plight. Before we have the right to speak of Christ to the world, we must exhibit his compassionate heart and redemptive activity.

Ministry to those who are sick must be offered "with no strings attached," if it is to model Jesus to others. Philippians 2 emphasizes Christ's self-emptying spirit as the model for his followers. Without approving or disapproving a person and/or her lifestyle, we move to restore her to health and wholeness. Without needing to judge whether a person came to his plight because of circumstances beyond his control or because "he is getting what he deserves," we affirm him as a valuable human being who is created in the image and likeness of God. We thus demonstrate to all who receive our aid or observe it being given that we have been with Christ. We love without keeping score. We approach the world not with clinched fists or in a defensive posture but with a practical demonstration of Christ-imitating compassion. "Therefore, as we have opportunity, let us do good to all people, especially to those who belong to the family of believers" (Gal. 6:10).

The Wider Circle of Concern
As Paul indicates, the church has a special responsibility to its own. But we should not overlook his Spirit-guided counsel that the church is to do good to all people. So a church's leadership must avoid the temptation to be so internally focused that it fails

to bless people who are not part of its congregational life. From a history that often has been isolationist, Churches of Christ must also avoid the temptation to neglect persons from other Christian groups, non-Christians in our increasingly diverse communities, and people who are hostile to religion in any form.

For example, Christ-like leadership in our churches will be involved in efforts to make health care accessible to people who need it. There is a health care crisis in the United States that most of us know through people in our own churches. Health insurance is a practical necessity to all of us, but many people do not have access to it. Premiums are so high that many small companies do not offer it to their employees. For many people in entry-level jobs, they cannot afford to have the premiums deducted from their wages with companies that offer elective health care coverage. More and more large companies are "out-smarting" the system by hiring part-time rather than full-time workers in order to avoid the obligation of providing coverage. An underclass of persons and families has been created that is known as "the working poor." They earn enough to keep a roof over their heads and food on the table, but they cannot afford basic health care for the adults and children in those house-holds. They make too much to qualify for government-provid-ed health care; they make too little to purchase either health care insurance or to pay for medical services at standard rates.

We are in a near-impossible situation for many people. Because they cannot afford primary health care (that is, routine checkups, doctor visits for chronic problems such as hyperten-sion, mammograms, etc.), they get treatment only after some dis-ease has manifested with well-developed symptoms (for example, heart attack, advanced cancer). Costs now are higher. Treatments are less effective. And the fragile economy of that family col-lapses. The escalation sometimes continues and compounds itself through depression, alcoholism, and other debilitating conse-quences. For these same families in a less-severe crisis such as an automobile accident, work-related injury, or severe illness, the primary resource available to them in many communities is a hospital emergency room. The care is excellent, but the costs are highest. Either the family's budget goes bust or others pay for the emergency room visit through higher taxes and higher health insurance premiums.

I do not know how to solve this country's crisis in health care. What I do know, however, is that our churches can learn to participate with people in various communities to do something that makes a difference. For the moment, let's not talk public policy debates but community activism with our churches involved rather than sitting on the sidelines.

Most cities of any size have non-profit groups that have formed to do something for people such as the ones I have just described. Often the initiative has been taken by people of faith to provide basic health services for people outside the loops of either government-provided health care for the very poor or private-insurance health care for the more affluent. That in-between category of "working poor without health care" is being served in Nashville, for example, by Faith Family Medical Clinic. Strongly supported by local hospitals, this excellent clinic sees patients at an average cost of $10 to $30 for an office visit that may well include blood work and x-rays. Physicians, hospitals, business persons, churches, and generous individuals make its services possible. Why should we be distant from those works? Because we did not think of them first? Because we do not have control of them? Or because we do not take compassion for the sick seriously enough?

There is another option for helping people with serious health problems that requires no medical specialists or health clinics. Non-professional support groups meet by the thousands across the United States every day. Most of them are built on the highly successful model of Alcoholics Anonymous. These twelve-step groups deal with issues ranging from alcohol and drugs to obesity and smoking. God is going to hold some church leaders accountable for the six-hour per week use of expensive church buildings that could have been made available for a variety of purposes that would have made their communities better. With regard to a church's imitation of Jesus' care for the physically, emotionally, and spiritually ill, church leaders can make classrooms and fellowship rooms available to these groups. Don't wait for them to call you. Go to the phone book, look up Alcoholics Anonymous, and pass the word that you have space available. Make an announcement to your members about it. Let the word go out that you care about the general well-being of people—not just their enrollment in your Bible classes or attendance in your Sunday assemblies.

There are practically limitless options for a church to partner with community groups to help others without feeling any sense of compromise of the unique Christian identity and message we are privileged to carry. Are there agencies who seek foster and adoptive parents? Is there a shelter for abused women and children? Is someone forming care teams for persons with AIDS? Is there a Suicide Prevention Hotline that needs volunteers? What about a ministry to women dealing with unwanted pregnancy? Or a ministry to women dealing with guilt and remorse over aborting an unwanted child? These are legitimate areas of concern and ministry to which churches should give publicity and in which men and women may serve as Christ's agents to help make persons whole. At the very least, a church can show its concern for the general well-being of its community by using its property and resources for such things as health fairs, blood drives, and the like.

Romans 8 envisions creation being rescued from the "futility" and "bondage to decay" that have been imposed by sin. The Old Testament speaks of the total sense of human well-being entailed in God's *shalom*. The church must bear witness to these divine passions in doing positive things for the good of all who know us. And one of the obvious places where we can make a contribution in this generation is within the wide circle of concern for all our neighbors. It is a way to obey the Pauline injunction to "do good to all people."

A Narrower Circle of Influence

Yet Paul acknowledged that the Christian community will be most aggressive and most effective in doing good works "to those who belong to the family of believers." In this narrower circle of ministry, church leaders have a special opportunity and responsibility to their brothers and sisters in the Lord Jesus Christ. Our wider circle of concern for the sick and bruised is illustrated by the Parable of the Good Samaritan, in which the "hero" cares for one outside his own religious and cultural group. The fact remains that the narrower circle of importance to us will be our own Christian family.

"Orthodoxy" is a term practically everyone knows. It signifies *correct belief.* "Orthopraxy" points to *correct actions.* It is not our option to choose between these two but to embrace both. The apostle John, for example, wrote extensively about orthodox doctrine (cf. 2 John 7-9). But he also wrote of orthopraxy. "If anyone says, 'I love God,' yet hates his brother, he is a liar. For anyone who does not love his brother, whom he has seen, cannot love God, whom he has not seen" (1 John 4:20). Within the local church, we may minister to one another in a variety of ways.

Church leaders should certainly take the lead in teaching material of the sort contained in the first half of this essay. Christ must be seen as the Compassionate Shepherd of his flock, if the flock is to follow his example. Sermons, classes, and written materials featured in the life of a church establish both content and tone for its people. One of the most persistent issues with which believers need help is the one already raised about the connection of illness, accident, and physical suffering with the

will of God. The myth still prevails that people do not suffer
unless God wills it, that suffering is necessarily linked to one's
punishment from the divine hand.

Pastoral teaching and counseling must constantly remind people that human circumstances have never been a reliable index
either to a person's spiritual status in the eyes of God or to his or
her value to God. For more than a dozen years, Joseph was either
a slave or a prisoner in a country where he had no civil rights and
no legal protection. By the calculus of some, anything beyond a
few days or weeks of suffering would be taken as solid proof that
God had abandoned Joseph. Tamar was raped. Ruth's husband
died—and she had to fend for herself in a male-dominated culture. Suffering Lazarus was a pious man, and the rich man at
whose gate he begged was impious and insensitive; death revealed that their spiritual status was hardly indicated by their
health and general welfare on planet earth. Prophets and martyrs
across millennia have been put in dungeons, thrown to wild animals, and forced to watch their children be murdered.

It is important to treat this theme with regularity. Otherwise
Satan tempts people to compound their physical pain with spiritual despair. There is simply no correlation between one's circumstance on a given day and God's faithful love. Like the
Israelites in the wilderness, that situation may be only a period
of discipline prior to entering the Promised Land. Like Paul's
thorn in the flesh, it may be one's invitation to experience God's
grace at a deeper level.

When considering ministry to sick persons by church leaders,
we are also confronted with this text from the New Testament:

> Is any one of you sick? He should call the elders of the
> church to pray over him and anoint him with oil in the
> name of the Lord. And the prayer offered in faith will
> make the sick person well; the Lord will raise him up. If
> he has sinned, he will be forgiven. Therefore confess

your sins to each other and pray for each other so that you may be healed. The prayer of a righteous man is powerful and effective. (James 5:14-16)

It is clear that the original context envisions something very different from a call for public confession of sins. This is a private setting to which elder–shepherds of a given city have been called to the home of a sick person. James envisions their ministry to the physical and spiritual welfare of the person involved. While anointing him or her with oil, they are to pray for healing. While attending to physical welfare, they are to be most especially sensitive to the person's spiritual welfare. Within the confines of the sick room, confession and prayer for forgiveness may be even more urgent than prayers for healing. This would be especially so in cases where a person was dying. In both first- and twenty-first-century settings, it is appropriate to ask God to bring physical healing; it is even more appropriate for a church's spiritual leaders to counsel and encourage one to receive spiritual healing.

Although many churches have put the responsibility for visiting and praying for the sick on paid staff, leadership in this ministry belongs to elder–shepherds of local churches. In hospitals and in private homes, intercessory prayer should be a major ministry of the church. If there are regular elder meetings, perhaps one hour before those meetings could be devoted to prayer for the sick and discouraged. With a minimum of congregational awareness, people will begin to come to these settings in person for prayer. Occasionally elders may choose to lead pastoral prayers for the sick, distressed, and hurting in public assemblies as well. This not only fulfills a biblical commission but also establishes great moral and spiritual authority within the body.

It is not possible within the space of this essay to consider all of the possible scenarios involving illness, caregiving, and modern medical technology that conscientious Christians may bring to a church's leadership for counsel as well as prayer. But a common and growing concern in churches of all backgrounds and sizes has to do with end-of-life issues and treatment decisions involving terminal illness. While Christian men and women generally respect and are inclined to defer to the counsel of medical professionals, they will often—whether formally or informally—test their thinking and solicit the advice of their spiritual leaders.

That is why Mark Burress called me within a few hours of the word he received and took home to Melanie. So we met the following Monday to begin processing information and sharing a remarkable journey of faith. How to tell his parents the news he had been given? How to deal with his anxiety as a believer? What to do with the questions and anger swirling through his head? We talked about John 9. And we began a partnership larger than the two of us that took a whole church family into his confidence and on his pilgrimage.

Until the last century, most people died suddenly from accidents, infections, and diseases diagnosed only in their advanced stages. The average life expectancy of both black and white males, for example, increased by approximately 30 years between 1900 and 2000. This is traceable to modern diagnostic imaging advances (for example, x-ray, CAT scan), vastly improved surgical interventions (for example, coronary bypass surgery), antibiotics, and the like. Now most people are likely to die in old age and to live an estimated two to five years with serious illness.

Along with many other issues created by this paradigm shift, concerns for the dignity, self-determination, and degree of care appropriate at the end of life emerge. This essay is not concerned to evaluate ethical issues on which widespread agreement among persons in our religious tradition is found (for example, suicide, active euthanasia) but to consider only those cases which now occur with frequency in which injury or disease has made death both inevitable and imminent. While the general rule in making ethical decisions concerning any living organism with a human genetic code should be in favor of its preservation, it is a quantum leap to insist that nothing be spared to maintain someone's heart and respiration. Families often seek spiritual counsel from their church leaders about the degree of care necessary for someone dying of Alzheimer's disease, massive head trauma following an automobile accident, or advanced cancer. From Karen Ann Quinlan to Terri Schiavo to Susan Torres, the public debate over the degree of care appropriate to persons unable to recover has also been engaged by morally sensitive persons in our churches.

Not only physicians and ethicists but the rest of us are discerning enough to know there is a profound difference between protecting, enhancing, and empowering a human life with reasonable hope of recovery and merely prolonging the process of dying. Skill and technology that do the former are admirable and ethical; the same skill and technology used for the latter are unnecessary and ill-advised.

In what medical literature calls a "persistent vegetative state" (PVS), higher brain function has ceased. Some diseases and certain types of head trauma leave patients comatose and essentially non-responsive. Others, however, are not comatose but may spontaneously move their limbs, experience wake-sleep cycles, and make sounds. Their eyes may open in response to external events. PVS persons may occasionally grimace, cry, or laugh. As with coma patients, however, there is no cognitive engagement with their environment. People who have no experience with such persons—and persons with emotional attachments to them—typically find it difficult to accept that he or she lacks the ability for rational thought or conscious expression. Random moves and noises or responses to external stimuli are counted as signs the person is "still there."

Because there is no single, unquestioned quantitative test for PVS (for example, brain scan, EEG, etc.), the diagnosis is typically made over a period of time during which a patient is observed carefully. Long-term preservation of these persons may involve a range of interventions from hydration and feeding tubes to breathing devices to electrical stimulation of heartbeat. In such instances, death is not "the ultimate enemy" and is not always to be resisted. The real enemies to the patient are disease, trauma, degeneration, and unnecessary pain. Proxy decision-makers are able to take these things into account in a way persons in a persistent vegetative state cannot. A key issue here is our common insensitivity that fails to see that what is *best* for a person lacking higher-brain function is not always the *most* that is possible. In orthodox Christian theology, death certainly is not an absolute evil. It is sometimes an instrumental good for those without reasonable hope of recovery. Sometimes the real evil lies in forcing someone to endure existence that is no longer really life in any meaningful sense.

Because these are such personal decisions and often are made within the context of confused family dynamic, the role of church leaders may be most helpful in listening more than speaking, clarifying ethical issues rather than offering judgments about them, and giving families prayerful support as they wrestle through heartaches involved in such situations. Again, whatever time and counsel are invested with such persons and families must involve great humility, kindness, and compassion.

In occasional educational settings (for example, four-week class on "Contemporary Issues in Ethics," advertising a seminar offered by a local hospital), church leaders can do a great service for a congregation by providing information on such legal instruments as a Living Will or Durable Power of Attorney for Health Care. Most states have standard forms for these documents that allow persons to declare their wishes about end-of-life medical care such as being kept alive on machines, receiving artificial nourishment and hydration, and/or donating one's organs for transplantation in the event of a terminal medical condition where there is no reasonable medical hope for recovery.[5] Even in cases where documents are not executed, family discussions that allow persons to declare (before witnesses) their wishes and intentions can be very helpful in resolving crisis situations that eventually arise.

Elders, preachers, teachers, and other spiritual advisors are just that and no more—*advisors*. We may help individuals and families to process information. We may be part of a helpful interaction with medical professionals that helps persons and groups give "informed consent" to health care decisions. But the locus of ethical–spiritual decisions remains with the patient and/or patient surrogates (that is, family members, persons designated by a patient's Durable Power of Attorney for Health Care).

In times of crisis around sickness, our ministry is important as spiritual support and encouragement. It often becomes a time where spiritual clarification comes to many parties about the transience of life, fragility of health, importance of family ties, and need for a closer relationship with God. To miss these opportunities for service would be to fail those who have trusted us to provide spiritual leadership for their lives. To seize these opportunities is surely to minister in the name of Jesus.

CONCLUSION

After December of 1999, Mark and Melanie Burress lived their confident and confusing, faithful and frightened battle with leukemia in spiritual partnership. Ken and Ginger were along for the ride—with their good friends Barbara and Prentice Meador. The Prestoncrest Church of Christ in Dallas and the Family of God at Woodmont Hills were extended family to them all. But I'm getting ahead of myself in telling a story that isn't mine.

There were physicians at Vanderbilt University Medical Center and information downloads from the Internet. There would be trips to specialists in Minneapolis and Houston and Portland. There would be a bone-marrow donor drive sponsored by the

Brentwood Rotary Club in April of 2000 in the Woodmont Hills building. A 400-donor target became an overwhelming 1,400 donors that day! The Burresses were speechless to see how many people cared about their battle. No match for Mark was found that day, but six matches for other people did turn up within a matter of weeks—and several more since then. A similar bone-marrow donor drive was held at Prestoncrest. There was Interferon, STI-571, and so much prayer.

There was also pain and vomiting and anxiety. My electronic calendar logs not only days and hours for our meetings to talk and pray together but entries like "fast and pray for Mark," "take skydive and New Arrivals video to Mark," and "Burress family at elder meeting for prayer." There's also an entry that reads "Mark Burress about funeral plans." I have never seen anyone who handled his illness, suffering, and death with more clarity, faith, and hope than Mark did. When he died at his home on August 7, 2002, his wife was lying beside him in bed. His parents and four or five of us who were privileged to be his close friends were ringed around them singing, reading favorite biblical texts, and praying for God to send angels to bear him to Paradise.

At Mark's request, I read some short notes from him at his funeral. He wrote his parents, his wife, and his church family over the final few weeks he was with us. Here is what he wrote his daughter:

> To my wonderful daughter, Gracie: I guess I worry about you the most of all. You will have to live the rest of your life without your daddy and I know that is going to be very difficult. I also know that is not what we, your mommy and I, ever dreamed for you. You just don't go into having children thinking this sort of thing can happen.
>
> Gracie, cancer took my life. God did not take my life. Instead God surrounded me with His love and His

angels. He nurtured my spirituality and has walked me towards heaven. He will always do the same for you if you ask Him. I think the answer to all of your questions that you have and that we all have will come when you get to heaven. So I just encourage you throughout your life to stay focused on Jesus and I know you will have a wonderful life.

Mark was correct. The questions we have about the daddies of three-year-olds dying of leukemia or infants being born blind don't all get answered here. We live by our trust in God, not by a full supply of answers! But he is also correct in affirming that God surrounds us in our weakness and frailty with his love—in the form of people who care as Jesus did. And that is our challenge as his disciples in the churches that worship in his name.

He defended the dignity of the man who had been blind from birth. He neither added to his pain nor allowed others to do so with their ignorance. Instead, he told his disciples that their task was always to seize opportunities for helping souls in pain. We are imitating Jesus when we hear his instruction, model his compassion, and teach others to delight in doing so.

NOTES

1. Citations from the biblical text in this chapter are from the *New International Version*, unless otherwise specified. Copyright (c) 1973, 1978, 1984 by International Bible Society.

2. Quoted here from Eugene Peterson, *The Message* (Colorado Springs, CO: NavPress, 2002).

3. Even so, Jesus showed compassion to persons whose situations appear to have been due to their sinful behaviors. Cf. John 5:14.

4. *New Living Translation.* Copyright (c) 1996 by Tyndale Charitable Trust.

5. Legal documents to communicate advance directives about end-of-life care vary from state to state. Standard templates are available online by typing the name of one's state and terms such as "living will" and "durable power of attorney" into a search engine. Basic information on the key terms in these documents and their value may be found at http://www.mayoclinic.com/invoke.cfm?objectid=83E7580F-6506-4D06-B9424AC6ED1CA79A

BIBLIOGRAPHY

Works cited below are listed in order of their complexity and readability. The first several are written from the standpoint of Christian commitments, whereas the latter ones provide information for those who may wish to pursue specific topics in medical ethics from a broader perspective.

Nouwen, Henri. *Can You Drink the Cup?* Notre Dame, IN: Ave Maria Press, 1996. Nouwen deals with the broad issue of the spiritual life and treats the place of suffering and ministry to those who suffer. This is an excellent challenge to the development of a pastoral heart in dealing with others.

Brueggemann, Walter. *The Threat of Life: Sermons on Pain, Power, and Weakness.* Minneapolis: Fortress Press, 1996. Written in the spirit of the Nouwen book, Brueggemann offers helpful teaching insights into several Old and New Testament texts that can aid in developing sermons, articles, and other teaching materials for a church.

Hauerwas, Stanley. S*uffering Presence: Theological Reflections on Medicine, the Mentally Handicapped, and the Church.* Notre Dame, IN: University of Notre Dame Press, 1986. A non-technical introduction to Christian ethics in relation to medicine. He explores some ways in which the church can interact with the community of those who are suffering in order to be the presence of Christ for them.

Stassen, Glen H., and David P. Gushee, *Kingdom Ethics: Following Jesus in Contemporary Context.* Downers Grove, IL: InterVarsity Press, 2003. A serious study of biblical grounding for ethical reasoning. Working from the Sermon on the Mount, Stassen and Gushee provide helpful insights on applying Scripture to contemporary issues, including bioethics.

Chouinard, Larry; David Fiensy; and George Pickens. *Christian Ethics: The Issues of Life and Death.* Joplin, MO: Parma Press, 2003. These essays serve as an introduction to Christian ethical theory by writers from Churches of Christ and Independent Christian Churches. Social, family, and medical ethics are treated in separate sections.

Foreman, Mark W. *Christianity and Bioethics: Confronting Clinical Issues.* Joplin, MO: College Press, 1999. Written from the perspective of an evangelical Christian, Foreman treats abortion, euthanasia, physician-assisted suicide, and treatment of imperiled newborns.

Beauchamp, Tom L., and James F. Childress. *Principles of Biomedical Ethics,* 5th ed. Oxford: Oxford University Press, 2001. A standard and widely used college textbook on issues in medical ethics. Not written from a Christian worldview.

Mappes, Thomas A. and David DeGrazia. *Biomedical Ethics,* 6th ed. New York: McGraw-Hill, 2005. A standard and widely used college textbook on issues in medical ethics. Not written from a Christian worldview.

AMA Council on Ethical and Judicial Affairs. *Code of Medical Ethics 2004-2005: Current Opinions with Annotations.* Chicago: American Medical Association, 2004. For use by medical professionals and academics. A reference guide on issues in medical ethics produced by the American Medical Association.

Chapter 5

MOVING TO THE RHYTHMS OF CHRISTIAN LIFE

Baptism for Children Raised in the Church

Jeff Childers

Parents soon realize that children are born without an appreciation for the value of money. Children come with many other things—sleepless nights, a persistent messiness, and a variety of loud noises that occur at the most inconvenient times—but they do not usually come with an inborn sense of the value of money. Kids typically presume that if checks are in the checkbook, a plastic card in the wallet, or ATMs on the street corner, mom and dad are being stingy if they guard their spending too closely. Yet in time even the most extravagant adolescents can evolve into shrewd spendthrifts once they become responsible for earning their own income. They learn to count because resources are limited.

Unfortunately for kids and parents alike, our consumer culture invites us to make commitments without counting the cost. When it comes to products and services, credit is easily available and prices are often given as "easy monthly payments" rather than actual costs. Furthermore, the advertisements always picture the most delightful and trouble-free experiences. Who would want to buy a product if the ads told the full and honest truth about the less savory side of ownership? Repair problems, bondage to debt, and the basic inadequacy of material things to satisfy our true spiritual needs—these are pictures that would blemish the airbrushed face of an otherwise compelling advertisement.

Perhaps for the same reason the church struggles with Jesus' advice to count the cost. Naturally, we want people to commit to Christ, to take on the Christian life, and to become a part of his church. We hope to attract outsiders and we especially hope to hang on to our own kids. If in our church "marketing" we were to lead with some of Jesus' harshest and most challenging statements, we might frighten away prospective newcomers— and we might have a harder time hanging onto the people that we already have. Yet shiny packaging and glossy incentives were foreign to Jesus' preaching of the Kingdom:

> "If anyone would come after me, he must deny himself and take up his cross and follow me." (Matt. 16:24)

> "If anyone comes to me and does not hate his father and mother, his wife and children...yes, even his own life— he cannot be my disciple." (Luke 14:26)

> "Suppose one of you wants to build a tower. Will you not first sit down and estimate the cost to see if you have enough money to complete it?....Or suppose a king is about to go to war against another king. Will he not first sit down and consider whether he is able...? In the same way, any of you who does not give up everything she has cannot be my disciple." (Luke 14:28-29, 33)

Discipleship slogans like these tend not to be the ones churches use today. These statements require an investment in Jesus' way, no holds barred. They promise hardship and sacrifice—even suffering. Perhaps this is why they are not prominently featured on churches' website mastheads, informational brochures, or roadside marquees.

Always a proponent of truth-in-advertising, Jesus wasn't afraid to make it clear that the Gospel has certain moves centered in death and resurrection (see 1 Cor. 15:1-8). The Gospel's moves give it a kind of rhythm—a way of being that takes its cues from the example and teaching of Christ. As Jesus moved to this rhythm through his days of ministry in Galilee and Palestine, he invited people to join him in the same rhythm—to yield themselves, take up a cross, and pursue the glory of God and the service of others through personal self-denial. "Can you be baptized with the baptism I am to be baptized with?" (Mark 10:38), he asked those who thought that they wanted to follow him. He spoke of his suffering so that his disciples would realize that they must be fully immersed into the same rhythm of death-and-life begun by his own baptism. "You will be!" he declared, answering his own question. If they would be his disciples, baptism would have to become a way of life for them.

Paul also noticed that baptism into Christ is a picture of the Gospel. By stepping into baptism a person is stepping into the Gospel story and yielding herself to the same rhythms of death and resurrection (Rom. 6:3-10). She is stepping into a dance that proceeds according to the rhythms of death and life lying at the heart of discipleship. In the words of Robert E. Webber:

> When we enter into the waters of baptism, we enter into a divine connection with the suffering of Jesus and with his resurrection. We are brought into a pattern of life that is an actual identification with Jesus. Baptism is there fore not only an identification with Christ but a calling to live the baptized life. The calling which baptism symbolizes gives concrete form to our spirituality....[1]

Jesus calls people to follow him, surrendering in the name of Father, Son, and Spirit and being swallowed up into the mission of the kingdom as disciples. The essence of Christian baptism is deeper than the cleansing forgiveness of sins, the act of joining the church or the experience of personal renewal. The essence of Christian baptism is total identification with Jesus and his mission through self-denial according to the rhythms of the Gospel story.

CONVERSION OR CONTINUITY?
THE PROBLEM WITH FORCED REVIVALISM FOR THE CHURCH'S CHILDREN

Gospel rhythms of death-and-life help us prepare people for baptism. This is especially true for one group in particular: children raised as part of the church family. They often occupy a weird place with respect to preparation for baptism since frontier revivalism runs deep in Church of Christ DNA. Children raised in the church family, however, are not often good candidates for revivalist approaches. So much preaching in Churches of Christ has focused on sinfulness and the need to repent—to obey Christ in baptism in order to forgive sins and to begin living a new life. The language of "conversion" implies discontinuity—that a person's life was moving in a particular direction until it "converted," taking a sharp turn in a different direction. Revivalism sees baptism as the sharp turning point.

Preaching that emphasizes the importance of conversion is appropriate—perhaps more so than ever given the post-Christian society in which we find ourselves. However, I must admit that I feel uncomfortable trying to convince my eleven-year-old son that he must give up his reprobate life of sin. After all, he has been raised by Christians in a Christian environment, and has been practicing the ways of Jesus for years. Even in two or three years I doubt—indeed, I dearly hope—that there will be no need to persuade him to forsake debauched habits, confess the depths of depravity, and turn from hardened ways of shameful living. Yet this is precisely the sort of assumption that seems to guide the way we handle baptism for children raised in the church, as if baptism ought to mark their radical repentance and conversion just as it does for people long steeped in sin. Because of our revivalist traditions of crisis conversion we typically feel the need to create for our children a crisis conversion experience. We stage youth rallies or encampments and bring in speakers especially skilled at stirring up adolescent emotions. The aim is to get youngsters to repent and convert in a heartfelt way. In such a climate, it takes only one or two conversions to start a trend; soon, they fall like dominoes, swelling the number of camp baptisms to a respectable level.

I realize that all people become sinners and need forgiveness. But to treat children preparing for baptism as if the only way to get ready is by owning up to their sinfulness is to ignore a basic truth: that *different people come to baptism in different ways*. This was as true in the first century as it is today. The idolatrous Gentile who was accustomed to an immoral life experienced baptism quite differently than the law-abiding Jew who had been long expecting the coming of Messiah's kingdom and was accustomed to his people's washing rituals. Similarly, for some today baptism represents a radical change of direction. Some have undergone genuine conversion and their baptisms mark the complete redirection of their lives.

But for others, baptism is the next step on a journey they have long traveled. The momentum of their lives carries them to the point of immersion in Christ before their church family. Their baptism is no less significant, but the role it plays in the Gospel story for them is different than it is for the person experiencing a complete redirection of life. For this person there is continuity in their journey with the Lord and his people. Most children raised in Christian homes come to baptism in this way. This way more nearly describes what I hope for my eleven-year-old son, more so than an experience of "conversion." I hope and pray that the day will soon come when he is ready to take on Christ in baptism. That will be a wonderful day and I plan to do all I can to ensure that he experiences the vitality of his baptism and cherishes it forever. But baptism will have a different meaning for him than it would for someone converting to Christ out of a life of sin.

A serious problem arises when we try to force everyone into the same baptismal mold—the revivalistic mold designed for non-Christians who are in need of fervent repentance and conversion. Some of our adolescents get to such a point, but many do not. Yet often they are all made to feel as if they must and under that pressure they may come to believe that they are at such a point when in fact they are not. With a revivalistic understanding of salvation as a total package delivered once-for-all it follows naturally that everything can appear to hinge on this all-or-nothing moment of emotional conversion and baptism. If in later years a person has doubts about the way he came to baptism, as often happens, he may question its validity. Or, when a person later goes through seasons of spiritual growth or has fresh "aha!" moments of new insight, she may come to question the authenticity of her earlier "conversion" and baptism. She has no way to make sense of natural spiritual growth because she has not been taught to see her spiritual life as an ongoing journey. In both of these circumstances, the people involved may have little choice but to consider rebaptism, claiming that they did not really understand what they were doing or that they have undergone some dramatic change since then. Rebaptism can be legitimate, but it has happened far too often in our churches, mainly because we have not helped people learn to expect seasons of growth, change, and even repentance and redirection in their Christian lives after baptism. We have not helped them see that baptism fits into our spiritual lives as part of the journey, not the sum total of our salvation.

Another problem with forcing everyone into a revivalistic pattern of conversion is that it tends to equate salvation with a certain kind of experience, mainly emotional, implying that everybody must have a similiar experience. For my part, I have always felt a little cheated. Some people are able to deliver stunning testimonies about their lost state prior to conversion. Given over to riotous living, they were rescued from the brink of self-destruction by alcohol or drugs, abusive homes, gangs, or satanism. In their harrowing narratives you really see the power of God to deliver the sinner. Sadly, I did not engage in any such colorful activities. Of course, I have (and still do) struggle with various kinds of sinfulness, every bit as vile and destructive. Yet I have no really juicy stories about being brought back from the brink of certain doom. For the most part, the narrative of my growing-up years is a drab tale involving a stable home life, godly parents, a nurturing and supportive church family, solid Bible teaching, and deliberate training in Christian discipleship from a very early age. The person brought up to revere the crisis conversion model may well ask: Where is the power of God in all that?

An ironic question. If the only valid story of coming to faith is crisis conversion, then some people will feel compelled to make up a suitable story or they will have to accept a kind of spiritual second-class status. I once envied people who offered sensational testimonies of dramatic rescue. Over time I have learned that God does not prefer to have to rescue people from the brink. He does so, thankfully, but it is not his preference. God's preferred way of bringing people to baptism is through the reliable, natural, and healthy processes created in the beginning, ones that happen in a nurturing family of faith, starting at an early age. God wishes everyone could have that sort of experience. Yet because of the traditional revivalist climate and the premium we put on crisis conversion we rarely showcase such "bland" stories of faith. This is troubling. If our habits of testimony and of bringing people to baptism are so focused on *conversion* that we make our kids wish they could get some real sin under their belts in order to show that their faith is genuine, we have a serious problem.

BELIEVERS' BAPTISM VS. INFANT BAPTISM

Here is where we could learn from the practice of infant baptism. Let me clarify: I am not saying that infant baptism is preferable. What I mean is that those who practice infant baptism often emphasize different biblical themes than those of us committed to believers' baptism. We who practice believers' baptism tend to emphasize the importance of the adult faith and commitment that Jesus requires of his disciples. Those who practice infant baptism tend to see more clearly the Bible's teachings about children's place in the church. Comparing the two will help us notice some biblical themes that we cannot afford to ignore.

Practitioners of believer's baptism tend to emphasize the faith of the individual. Each person takes responsibility for his or her own life. A woman stands before God as an individual and makes her own commitment to the Lord; no one can do it for her. By submitting to baptism she demonstrates her own understanding, personal faith, and willing surrender to Christ. *Practitioners of infant baptism tend to emphasize the faith of the community.* The church family plays a crucial role in preserving the Gospel and passing it on to the next generation. The faith of the entire group is in play, since without it there would be no teaching, no nurturing, no baptism. There is a strong sense that children belong to the church family from birth.

Practitioners of believers' baptism tend to emphasize the place of human responsibility in salvation, stressing the importance of a person's conscious, individual response to God. A man exerts some effort to obey God. Those who practice believers' baptism may be more keenly aware of the human element in the relationship between God and people. *Those who practice infant baptism tend to emphasize God's initiative in salvation.* Since a baby is helpless and totally dependent on the group, infant baptism reminds those who practice it that much of what shapes a soul towards God is outside that soul's control. Again, this prods them to look to community as a location for faith and God's activity.

Another distinction relates to worldview and the understanding of church in society. Generally speaking, *infant baptism presumes a Christian society*, or perhaps a Constantinian vision, one in which Christian identity is presumed for just about everybody. Like circumcision in ancient Israel, infant baptism tends to support the notion that everyone in a society will be a person of Christian faith simply by virtue of being born into that society. This "Constantinian" vision of church in society is one of several factors that helped cement the practice of infant baptism into the Christian tradition of Late Antiquity and the Medieval era. *Believers' baptism,* by contrast, *presumes the need for a community set apart from the world.* It helps create and sustain the sense that God calls people out of a sinful world to a changed life and an alternative community. Obviously, the Constantinian vision of church in society is becoming very difficult to sustain in our increasingly post-Christian world. Our society is a mission field, and a mission field invites believers' baptism.

Other comparisons could be made, but these three items illustrate significant differences. I strongly advocate believers baptism for biblical, historical, and missional reasons. Yet I cannot help but notice that we are sometimes so focused on the adult conversion model that we tend to miss two biblical themes that could help us raise our children in the Lord:

1) *Faith is not merely an individual commodity.* By studying Israel and the early church we learn that the faith of the community counts. Individual faith never stands alone; it begins and develops within the experiences and commitments of the faithful group. This leads us to emphasize the role of the church family in forming faith in children.

2) *Children belong to the family of faith, even before baptism.*
Children raised within the church family are not simply outsiders. The vision of community in the Old Testament obviously
includes the children, and in the New Testament we see God's
heart for children and God's conviction that they belong fully to
his people:

> "Let the little children come to me, and do not hinder
> them, for the Kingdom of heaven belongs to such as
> these" (Matt. 19:14)

> "The promise is for you and your children...." (Acts 2:39)

> ...bring them up in the training and instruction of the
> Lord. (Ep. 6:4)

> The unbelieving wife has been sanctified through her
> believing husband. Otherwise your children would be
> unclean, but as it is, they are holy. (1 Cor. 7:14)

Whatever else may be said about Paul's somewhat cryptic statement in 1 Corinthians 7:14, he clearly believes that children of
a Christian parent enjoy inclusion in God's community. God
wants us to see our children as belonging to the family of faith—
not as outsiders. This is not to say that there is no difference
between the baptized and the unbaptized, but the difference
cannot be one of insider/outsider that the revivalist tradition
presupposes.

We tend to show some very good instincts about this. We
stress the importance of church as family and we strive to find
ways for our kids to feel a part of it. Yet we also believe that
there is a difference between the baptized and the unbaptized
and that it is our responsibility to prepare our children for baptism. We struggle to answer the question, When is a child ready
for baptism?

HEAD, HEART, AND LIFE COMMITMENT—A WAITING GAME

Traditionally in Churches of Christ, answering the question of readiness has depended on knowledge. Does a person *know* enough of the right data? Does she understand the facts of the Gospel and display a decent awareness of how salvation works? Can he say, "I believe Jesus is the Son of God" and have a good grasp of what that means? Is he aware of his sinful state and is he ready to rely on Jesus' ability to grant forgiveness? In this way of thinking, when a person shows a certain degree of knowledge and seems old enough to be accountable, he or she is ready.

This kind of knowledge is important but it is only a component of discipleship—probably not the larger part. In recent years we have seen more focus on the state of a person's heart. Does she love Jesus? Does he understand his need for Jesus and genuinely desire a deep and personal relationship with him? When they say, "I believe..." are they deeply sincere? And again, do they feel their sinfulness and are they moved to trust Jesus' ability to handle it? Are they adequately aware of their need to be accountable?

Increasing emphasis on the state of a person's heart partly accounts for recent moves toward younger baptisms. After all, very young children can know a surprising quantity of facts and systems. Even more, they can exhibit astonishing degrees of faith and love. Indeed, young children can instruct us who are older in the ways of committed *childlike* faithfulness. Yet if we have not helped them understand the place of baptism in their ongoing journey of faith, they may come to believe that baptism is the only and most natural way to express those first self-conscious urgings of love towards Christ.

Knowledge of the facts and sincerity of heart are both fundamental to discipleship. But when it comes to believers' baptism, knowledge and love provide only part of the picture—and not the larger part of what believers' baptism enacts. Believers' baptism, in contrast to infant baptism, requires a measure of *maturity.* In keeping with the New Testament picture of baptism as participation in a story and identification with Jesus, baptism entails a lifestyle commitment. As such it presupposes some experience with life and loss, some maturity, and an ability to think realistically about consequences. Its action embodies a person's joining Jesus in discipleship, stepping into a dance characterized by spending one's life moving with Kingdom rhythms of self-denial for the sake of the world.

My three children have always been a part of the Christian community of faith. My wife and I raised them as part of the church family. They have always believed in God. They have loved Jesus for a long time and been serving him in many different ways. They have long known the facts of the Gospel and understood much about Jesus. None of these items has ever been in question—but none of them signalled my children's readiness for baptism. Yet for the two oldest the time came when they were ready to adopt a particular way of life—the baptized way of life, the death-and-resurrection-with-Christ way of life. We had made it very clear to them what that lifestyle involved, both by teaching them and by ensuring that they got large tastes of that life regularly. Of course, we talked about sin and guilt and studied the subject of repentance, practicing disciplines of self-examination and confession. But for our children, raised in the church family, the subject of repentance and conversion could not supply the primary way of understanding what was happening in their lives at this crucial point. Instead, we focused on the journey that they had been on for some time, exploring the possibility and hope that the time had come for them to decide whether to take the step of baptism and thereby join Jesus' mission as a mature disciple.

Young children tend not to make such decisions. Young children in our churches can adore Jesus and want to serve him— they probably already are, maybe more passionately than many adults. They may feel called into a deep relationship with Christ at an early age. They may have a good grip on the facts of the Gospel. These are elements of childhood faith that we hope they will never lose. We can encourage them in their desire to seek God, affirming their sense of calling and belonging, reassuring them that they have a genuine relationship with the Lord and a valued place in his church. We can use every opportunity to point out to them the signposts showing that they are on the journey of faith with God's people. But we ought to be cautious about applying baptism as an act of devotion or as a way to deal with a child's developing consciousness regarding guilt or as a ceremony to validate their relationship with the Lord and their place in the church family. Ideally, baptism entails a deliberate entry into a certain kind of lifestyle—the "taking up a cross and humbling myself for the sake of others"-lifestyle, the "putting others first"-lifestyle. When a person begins to understand what that lifestyle commitment means, elements of her childhood faith flow into the mature faith that believers' baptism enacts so that she is ready to surrender her life to join Jesus' mission.

Several years ago, my son declared that he wanted to be baptized. I warmly affirmed him, asking him to describe why. He explained that he wanted to be baptized so that he could share the Lord's Supper with the church every Sunday—a wonderful aspiration. Yet when I probed the matter a bit more, I discovered that his desire to share the Lord's Supper stemmed from his regular experience of hunger during the morning worship time. Apparently, my son's opinion was that our preacher tended to speak too long. He reasoned that some access to snacks midway through the service would provide some relief. On this revelation I took the opportunity to explain that he might need to wait for baptism.

Sometimes waiting is not easy. Children want to feel as if they belong to the group and they can find it very difficult to wait for baptism, particularly if we have not done a good job helping them find their places in God's family. Still, the wisdom of many cultures shows us the value of disciplined waiting. In cultures that have rites of passage to mark the move from childhood to adulthood, these are highly treasured and formative experiences. Youth look forward to them with great anticipation and the experiences serve as benchmarks, powerfully shaping the person's identity and providing him with a signpost for the rest of his life. Baptism is meant to have just such a long-term, formative impact on a person's life.

There is no cruelty in guiding children to wait—not if it is the right sort of waiting. On the one hand, we can find ways of recognizing the pre-baptismal faith of children. On the other hand, we can retain the discipleship thrust and life-shaping impact of believers' baptism by helping children count the cost before they surrender to the lifestyle rhythms inherent in baptism. Two approaches can help us bring these impulses together: 1) a dynamic sense of salvation as a journey and 2) a communal notion of children's involvement in the church.

1) Dynamic Salvation
Capturing the Biblical Picture
The Gospel is not so much a set of principles that we obey as it is an unfolding story that we step into. Salvation is not so much a possession that we pocket as it is an ongoing relationship that we enjoy. As Paul said, we are *"being* saved" (1 Cor. 1:18). Salvation involves a lifetime of seeking to "attain to the measure of Christ" and grow "up into him who is the head" (Eph. 4:13, 15), of constantly "pressing ahead" to take on the shape of Jesus' life, death, and resurrection a little more each day (Philip. 3:10-14). This, more than even forgiveness or heaven, is the true aim of our salvation: "What we will be has not yet been made known. But we know that when he appears, we shall be like him..." (1 John 3:2). That is our goal—the new creation (2 Cor. 5:17). The Christian life is a process of moving toward that goal, as "we, who with unveiled faces all reflect the Lord's

glory, are being transformed into his likeness with ever-increasing glory..." (2 Cor. 3:18). According to the apostles, salvation is an ongoing experience of walking with the Lord, beholding him, and enjoying the changes that come as he shapes us into the people we were always meant to be.

The apostles' dynamic view of salvation puts baptism in a different light than revivalism tends to do. Baptism into the name of Jesus plays a crucial and defining role in connecting a person to Christ and fully involving her in the unfolding story of her salvation. But baptism is by no means the end—it is a beginning. Yet for children raised in the church family baptism is not strictly the beginning either, since we hope that those children have been enjoying a relationship with God long before baptism. This is where strictly static understandings of salvation and baptism let us down. In a frontier revival setting, categories of repentance and conversion make sense. Simple distinctions between *saved* and *lost* appear to work well. But these categories leave us badgered by certain kinds of questions: Is a person a member of the church or not? Are they redeemed or lost? If children are innocent at first, when are they no longer? When do they become responsible for their state and need to think about moving from *sinful* to *saved*, from outsider to insider? We may find ourselves stumped by the conundrums created by questions such as these, conundrums for which the Bible provides no simple, straightforward answers. A static view of salvation creates a kind of all-or-nothing logic that simply does not square with the truth of our experience or resonate with the full witness of Scripture.

Our experience invites us to use some discernment in the ways that we employ such narrow, either/or categories—especially since these categories tend not to provide helpful ways of talking about the place of children raised in the church family. The static, all-at-once idea of salvation is in tension with the long-term, developmental and more organic process we see at work in children who grow up as part of the church family, moving into deeper relationship with the Lord year after year, perhaps long before their baptisms. By teaching the biblical view of salvation as a dynamic process we can help our children situate their relationship with God in a process of steady growth rather than perpetuating the false view that they should picture themselves merely in terms of in-or-out, saved-or-not.

We can also help our children by teaching them the language of salvation. Language choice, over time, is a powerful means of transforming convictions and assumptions. For instance, we need not confine ourselves to the language of *member/non-member,* since *membership* is typically used in an unbiblical and institutional sense. Instead, talking in terms of church as *body* recovers the biblical notion of membership. Also helpful is the kinship language of *family,* along with the language of *community,* since these terms involve relationship and an awareness of unity-in-diversity. *Disciple, discipleship,* and *following Jesus* are expressions that capture the image of a person in pursuit of Christ. Terms like *journey* and *growth* also help people picture a spiritual life on the move, one that passes through stages and experiences different seasons. The term *story* reminds us that each of us is part of a larger, unfolding narrative and that God works with his people over time. By percolating terms like these into a church's language, more dynamic understandings of salvation can take root deep in the consciousness of a congregation, understandings that reflect more accurately the organic ways that kids actually grow into faith.

Expressing Hope for the Future

Another way to help kids appreciate the process of moving into a grown-up faith is by regularly expressing hope for their futures. The way we talk to and about a child helps him see himself as a person already traveling down the path toward baptism. Even while we make it clear to our children that we hope they will one day make their own decisions for Christ, we can talk in terms of *when* rather than *if*. We want them to see baptism and committed discipleship as the natural outcome of their childhood identities. I have never said to one of my children, "*If* you graduate from High School..." or "*if* you live out on your own some day...." Instead, in both instances I use only *when*, hoping to create and sustain those healthy expectations for my children. Of course, we cannot condone the use of force when it comes to baptism—neither by applying parental pressure nor by the use of threatening preaching. Yet we make a serious mistake if, out of a desire not to prejudice our children, we do not bless them with the confident expression that their childhood devotion will one day flow into grown-up faith, baptism, and Christian service. Of all the expectations we lay on our children, this is by far the most crucial, especially when we do it in such a way that they feel blessed by our hope, not trapped by our manipulation.

Preparation and Pre-baptismal Instruction
Crisis conversion models of revivalism stress the value of sudden spiritual awakenings and bursts of conviction. Modern romantic impulses favor the sort of faith that comes as a private, interior, and primarily emotional experience. However, a dynamic view of salvation takes into account the developing process by which people can come to baptism. Although it may be tempting to underscore the apparent spontaneity of many conversions in the book of Acts, a closer look reveals that the picture is not so one-sided. Look at the Jews who were baptized in Jerusalem at Pentecost, the Ethiopian eunuch, or Cornelius—although we see some spontaneous elements in each instance, we greatly misconstrue what happened if we insist that the conversions were sudden and totally spontaneous. In each case, the people involved had long been engaged in preparation through their study of scripture, their association with God's people, and their developed expectations about God's coming kingdom. In each

case, baptism into Christ had more continuity than discontinuity with their religious lives.

The same is true for many kids raised in the church, reminding us that "baptism by surprise" is not the only valid kind of baptism. At home and in the church's educational programs we can incorporate *catechesis*—the ancient habit of conducting an intentional program of pre-baptismal instruction for learners in the faith. Every family and every church can develop the programs that suit them best. With my kids I have used our church's "Faith Foundations" statement as a basis for instruction. It outlines and summarizes key beliefs about God, salvation, the church, Scripture, baptism, the Christian mission, and so forth. Organized according to the persons of Father, Son, and Holy Spirit, it has served as a useful outline for pre-baptismal instruction. At the congregational level, our church has joined many other congregations in adapting Tommy King's outstanding "Faith Decisions"[2] curriculum for middle-schoolers. There are other published resources that can also be helpful. The content and delivery of the material ought to ensure not only that our children are being grounded thoroughly in basic Christian beliefs and practices but also that they are being brought to a point of readiness for making a mature baptismal commitment.

Affirming Everyday Signs of Growth

Another way to help children become more aware of their developing relationship with God is by regularly affirming signs of growth. Attentiveness to their words and actions pays off in opportunities to encourage and support their signs of spiritual maturity. In Bible classes, with small groups, in the home environment, and before the gathered church we find ample settings for openly noticing the faithful direction of our kids' lives and expressing our appreciation for their sacrificial contributions.

God sometimes works in delightfully surprising and spontaneous ways. But God more often transforms people through the normal, natural processes invented in the beginning. God even submitted to these processes, becoming a human child who grew in wisdom and stature in a first-century peasant home (Luke 2:52). When it comes to childhood faith it can be tempting to focus mainly on serendipitous experiences and sensational displays of spirituality. The concentrated, high-energy events that determine the basic contours of many Children's and Youth Ministries often provide impactful and transformative moments for the kids involved. However, they can also eclipse the even deeper impact that the less glamorous, weekly spiritual habits can have on a child's life. The regular, quiet disciplines and plain demonstrations of Christlikeness that we see in children on a daily basis actually provide better benchmarks for gauging genuine and lasting spiritual growth. Encouraging the classic disciplines of prayer, Bible reading, committed worship participation, regular fellowship, and acts of Christian service promote the kinds of natural processes that characterize healthy church ecologies. By affirming our kids' progress we inspire them to invest in habits that will become key to lifelong transformation.

2) Communal Involvement

Discipleship is not a solo experience. As community and family we move according to our Lord's rhythms of discipleship. For our kids the best dance instruction is experienced alongside other faithful followers at different places on the journey. In short, preparation for baptism involves raising children so that they are deeply connected to the larger church family. There are many ways to facilitate this.

Telling Children They Belong. Put simply, our children long to hear from us words declaring that they genuinely belong—at home, in Bible classes, and before the gathered congregation.

Children's Blessings. Many churches invite new parents to bring their babies before the congregation to lay hands upon them and pray over them, reinforcing that these newcomers are part of the family. The simple ritual clarifies the expectation that parents will raise their children in the Lord and that the people of the church are obligated to help. Some churches also take pains to present kids for blessing and prayer at key times in the children's lives, such as when they start school or at their graduations. Some groups of elders welcome families into their meetings to receive words of affirmation and prayer.

Showing Interest in Children. I love it when older members of the congregation show a genuine interest in the church's kids. One loving and attentive woman in our church scans the local newspaper every day, looking for any mention of a child she knows. Whenever one of our children has made the honor roll, won a prize for her entry at the county fair, or distinguished himself on an athletic team, she clips the article and sends it to us by mail. Some adults make it a point to attend the school, sports, and musical events of the church's children, even though the children are not their own—yet by their actions they are showing that those children really are their own, in the family of God. Habits like these help keep the lives of the church's children interwoven with the church's overall life.

Intentional Intergenerational Experiences. I appreciate the efforts that some church leaders are making to create more intergenerational experiences in their congregations. Multiple structures of our society push us to segregate people by age and interest groups so that we have age-specific classes and lots of special interest groups within the church (youth, singles, young marrieds, etc). This can be a useful strategy, but if it is the church's only strategy it greatly inhibits genuine spiritual growth. The model we see in Ephesians. 4:7-16 is one in which all the various parts of the body of Christ are being linked together. As the pieces move together, by ligament, joint, and tendon, the whole body "grows up into him who is the head." Spiritual maturation happens when the different parts are working, praying, eating, playing, and learning alongside one another—indeed, they teach and learn from each other. Segregating groups may be useful at times, but churches that genuinely desire to integrate children are finding creative ways to put people back together rather than surrendering to the fragmenting forces of society that tend to drive us apart.

Intergenerational Classes and Small Groups. Putting people back together isn't easy. But I appreciate some churches' extraordinary efforts to encourage older people to be involved in children's classes and home groups that include children in their activities. It is much easier for a small group to send children into another room for an "age-appropriate" activity while the grown-ups enjoy their time together. It is more *transformative* for everyone if the group will find ways to stay and grow together. Parents are often surprised at how much their children benefit from staying with the grown-ups, even with advanced subject matter. In these settings adults who confront the spiritual needs and contributions of the children are profoundly enriched.

Sharing Meals and Fellowship. More and more churches are attempting to recover old-fashioned meal times together, inviting people from the community to join them. Instinctively churches know that sharing meals together regularly is a powerful means of building community, learning to serve, and fortifying commitment to the Lord—especially when people of different ages and walks of life sit down together.

Intergenerational Testimony. Churches can design opportunities for children to hear testimony from the older people and congregational leaders. By sharing the stories of how they came to faith and by narrating their life experiences with God and the church, older Christians not only provide models of faithfulness for children but also create greater intimacy, openness, and mutual reliance between the generations. Children benefit from sensational stories of dramatic conversion but they also benefit from the stories of those who grew up in the church family and can talk to the experience of those who are doing the same today.

Intergenerational Ministry: Training in the Baptized Lifestyle.
In many churches people of different ages are teaming up for
ministry. Kids and grownups together visit and encourage persons in nursing homes or hospice. Churches design mission trips
and service efforts so that whole families and different age
groups can participate alongside one another. These efforts show
good communal instincts. Leaders work hard to ensure that the
children's and youth curricula include major service components
so that kids spend time working alongside adults for the benefit of others. Instead of trips to Six Flags, trips to do mission
work in the inner city; instead of pizza and video parties, parties where the kids mow widows' lawns or help out at the
church pantry or clean floors at the battered women's shelter or
pack up food for Meals on Wheels. Children and youth can be
surprisingly responsive to opportunities like these. As their
labors flow into the life of the larger church they learn that their
lives are charged with meaning and they see firsthand that joining Jesus entails surrendering to Christ-like service.

Hard work in the name of Jesus is excellent preparation for
baptism. When young children decide to be baptized, often the
experiences on which they base that decision are devotional
kinds of experiences. Baptism enables them to demonstrate
their faith and to express the love for Jesus that is swelling within them. But often the rhythms that believers' baptism most
enacts—the Gospel moves of sacrifice, suffering, and death—
make up little or no part of the actual experiences on which
children base a decision for baptism. Vital as it is, devotional
experience is not the basis of discipleship in the Gospel.
Children need discipleship modeling from us; they need some
honest "truth in advertising" about what the invitation to baptism involves. Nowhere do children get a better sense of baptism's commitment than when they stand alongside older
Christians who by their selfless service are moving to the baptismal rhythms of death-and-life. In other words, *we are*

preparing kids for baptism when we are training them in the baptized lifestyle.

Public Baptisms. Baptism is deeply personal but not private. It is a public testimony to faith, an incorporation into the body of Christ, an event for communal celebration. Over against the secularizing legacy of interior and privatized faith, many churches are strongly encouraging public baptisms. Being present and involved when others confess faith and are baptized into Christ has an enormous impact on children's pre-baptismal growth. Not every baptism must happen on a Sunday or before the whole church but meaningful public baptisms contribute to the robust faith development of a church's children. The public setting enables churches to invite the children down to the baptistry for a close-up view, or gather around the baptized to touch and bless. In one church the person doing the baptism asks the congregation whether they will support and pray for the person being baptized—they answer, "We will!" Some churches have celebratory meals together after the baptism or throw a party for the person baptized. Many churches organize their worship order around the event, perhaps involving the candidate in the worship planning. A proper dynamic understanding of salvation can relieve any anxiety about "putting off" for a time the baptism of a child raised in the church family.

Some churches help baptismal candidates prepare a covenant statement that expresses their understanding of what it means to be baptized into Christ, encouraging them to read it publicly and refer back to it periodically. Many churches give the baptized person a memento of the occasion—a cross, a certificate, a Bible, a work of devotional art—hoping that a "pile of stones" stacked at the river's edge will memorialize the moment (Joshua 4:1-9). Communal practices like these provide people with resources that can help them remain committed to the death-and-life rhythms of baptism each day.

CONCLUSION: TRUSTING THE GOSPEL

My daughter was baptized two years ago. That wonderful event came as the result of her own decision and involved intentional preparation. It came out of God's work on her heart that day—but also out of his graceful activity through the processes of preparation. That preparation included a focused study of Scripture and doctrine at home. It included a lifelong engagement in the worship, teaching, and other activities of our church. It included intentional (sometimes grudging) involvement in the church's many service opportunities. Working with children in inner city Ft. Worth, packing manna bags for the homeless, cleaning up yards for the elderly, writing notes for the sick, stocking shelves at the pantry downtown—activities like these made up her training in the baptized lifestyle, getting her ready for the rhythms of an incredible lifelong relationship with Christ.

As we stood in the baptistry, I explained before the gathered church that the momentum of her whole life had been leading up to this point and that she had always been an insider with respect to her church family. She felt the truth of that since her church had always treated her as part of the family. When the time came for her public confession I did not simply ask her the yes-or-no question, "Do you believe...?" but I invited her to explain to us what she believed. In front of her church family she described her faith, capping it off with the declaration that she was committing herself to "live my life for him, and show it in everything I do." We knew that she had a fair idea of what that would mean because she had been practicing that lifestyle for years. Yet we also tried to help her appreciate that she was embarking on a fresh phase of her life by using the ancient Christian tradition of dressing her in a brand-new outfit of clothes right after her baptism. And since that day we have seen her live out her baptismal commitment in ever deepening ways.

The task of Christian parents and church leaders is to cooperate with God in creating a spiritual ecology in which children can grow into the image of Christ. This summer I am teaching the fifth graders at our church; in the fall, I will teach the high school class again. As I step into those classrooms I try to remind myself that the goal is not just to get the kids baptized, much less just to see that they behave or that they are busy and happy. My goal is not even to help them realize how much God loves them, nor merely to see them develop a "personal relationship" with Jesus. None of these goals captures the essence of ministry to children and youth because none of them captures the dynamic rhythms of salvation. The goal that provides adequate direction for pre-baptismal instruction is the one that takes its cues from the momentum of salvation itself: to create an environment in which kids are becoming more like Jesus Christ. By training them in the baptized lifestyle within that environment we are preparing them for baptism.

When is a child ready for baptism? With believers' baptism there is no magic age, no precise formula for calculating a person's readiness. Each person takes responsibility for his or her own decision. The process is too complex for any formula. God and his Holy Spirit are involved, as are the child's family and their church. We hope that kids will make good and lasting decisions about their baptisms but we cannot control that decision, nor should we try. Yet God has chosen to make us partners in the process of helping a person discover his or her salvation. If we will 1) give kids a sense of belonging to the church family from the very beginning and 2) help them understand how their baptism fits into the unfolding, dynamic story of their journey with the Lord, there is every reason to believe that they will make very good decisions about baptism. We can trust that the gospel rhythms they have been practicing all along will flow into a lifelong dance of devotion and service before the Lord.

NOTES

1. Robert E. Webber, *Ancient-Future Faith: Rethinking Evangel-icalism for a Postmodern World* (Grand Rapids, MI: Baker, 1999), 110.
2. See annotated bibliography below.

BIBLIOGRAPHY

Childers, Jeff W., and Frederick D. Aquino. *Unveiling Glory. Visions of Christ's Transforming Presence.* Abilene, TX: ACU Press, 2003. This book explores the life, death, and resurrection of Jesus, attempting to draw the reader's attention to the "dynamic picture of the transform-ing relationship that can exist when the Lord's people are so attentive to him that they begin to reflect his character." Aimed at Churches of Christ in the twenty-first century, the book focuses on the need to reclaim the dynamic dimensions of Jesus' saving work. One chapter focuses on Christian baptism as a participation in the baptism of Jesus. The book includes a study guide for class use or personal reflection.

Childers, Jeff W., and Frederick D. Aquino. *At the River's Edge: Meeting Jesus in Baptism.* Abilene, TX: ACU Press, 2004. Adapting material pre-sented in the authors' book, *Unveiling Glory,* the pamphlet explores what it means to meet Jesus in the Jordan River to be immersed into the baptized lifestyle. Its aim is to help readers gain a deeper and richer appreciation of the importance of baptism by seeing how baptism fits into salvation and connects to daily life. The book includes a study guide for class use or personal reflection.

"Foundations of Faith" statement. http://www.highlandchurch. org/about/about.php?item=ff. Organized into three paragraphs dealing with God the Father, God the Son, and God the Holy Spirit, this out-line statement summarizes key tenets of biblical faith and practice. Though the statement is no substitute for scripture itself and it has been specifically crafted for the use of a particular congregation, it is a helpful starting point for those trying to build a curriculum of pre-baptismal instruction focused on fundamentals.

Hicks, John Mark, and Greg Taylor. *Down in the River to Pray: Revi-sioning Baptism as God's Transforming Work.* Siloam Springs, AR: Leafwood, 2004. "Baptism is more important than you think," they claim, "but not for the reasons you suppose." Engaging the heritage of Churches of Christ, the authors affirm the instincts of those who see baptism as a mere sign of salvation already received and those who treat it simply as a legal divide between the saved and lost—showing that both perspectives are flawed. The authors' capable handling of the biblical text draws both instincts together, showing how each fits into the more appropriate understanding that "baptism is God's transforming work and serves the divine goal of transformation." The book includes thoughtful discussion and practical suggestions.

Jeschke, Marlin. *Believers Baptism for Children of the Church.* Scottsdale, PA; Herald Press, 1983. The Mennonite author helps readers devoted to believers baptism understand the different ways that people come to baptism. "Children of the church," like Timothy, are not as likely to have radical conversion experiences but will grow naturally into mature appropriation and ownership of their community's faith. Rather than being made to feel inferior, they can enjoy the benefits of the "more excellent way" of faith formation. Baptism marks their move from childhood "innocence to the Christian way in adolescence." The book explores a number of foundational biblical contexts and deals with such practical matters as timing and rebaptism.

King, Tommy W. "Faith Decisions: Christian Initiation for Children of the Glenwood Church of Christ." D.Min. thesis. Abilene Christian University, 1994. One of the most regularly consulted unpublished doctoral theses, Tommy King's "Faith Decisions" represents a major attempt to build a theologically sound and practical curriculum of pre-baptismal instruction for children raised in Churches of Christ. Many churches have found it a useful starting point for designing catechesis, adapting its material for their own youth ministries and as a resource for families. Available through the ACU library.

McNichol, Allan J. *Preparing for Baptism: Becoming Part of the Story of the People of God.* Austin, TX: Christian Studies Press, 2001. This brief study is a catechesis—a course of prebaptismal instruction. It invites the candidate to consider joining the story of God's people, describing the basics of the story historically from creation up through contemporary church history. It also explains the beliefs and practices that are enjoined upon those who join the story in baptism.

Webber, Robert E. *Ancient-Future Faith: Rethinking Evangelicalism for a Postmodern World.* Grand Rapids, MI: Baker, 1999. The author discusses some of the challenges Christianity presently faces because of of recent so-called postmodern shifts, arguing that the church's best opportunity to witness faithfully in a postmodern climate requires a restoration of the essential faith of the early church, with Scripture as control and foundation. The book calls for a renewed emphasis on the role of baptism in salvation, worship, church life, and daily Christian life.

Chapter 6

BEFORE WE SPLIT

Mediating Conflict in the Church

Randy Lowry

A number of years ago I received a telephone call from Ted Engstrom, former president of World Vision International, the effective Christian relief organization that works throughout the world. Engstrom said, "Randy, I want you to come with me for a day as I meet with the executives of Christian ministries. I think you will find the experience instructive." So I drove a hundred miles to a hotel and walked into a room with about twenty-five Christian ministry leaders: heads of Christian, community service, and parachurch ministries. Mr. Engstrom, probably seventy-five years old at the time, sat at the end of the table and began a day long dialogue with these Christian ministry leaders. The question he asked them is the question I want you to consider. It is, "What keeps you up at night?"

The ministry leaders gathered around that hotel table were highly talented, skilled, and educated. But, for the first time in months or years of their work, they were in a safe place. They were not with their board members. They were not with all of those who depended on their organization for assistance or on whom their organization depended for support. They were with colleagues and the special friend sitting at the end of the table. He asked the question, "What keeps you up at night?" and they began to share.

As they conversed with one another, I watched what was happening. Here were people who were marvelous leaders, but in the safety of this moment, they began to reveal the struggles of their work and their lives. One would disclose what was going on in her organization and another would share his struggles as a parent, spouse, or Christian. For about six hours I listened to them openly describe, sometimes through frustration and tears, the difficult moments in their lives. At the end of the day, Mr. Engstrom told them how much he appreciated their work, gave them all a copy of his recent book on leadership, and prayed for them. With that, the day was over but what a blessing he had been in their lives. I had learned how important it is to have a strategy when dealing with the challenges that confront us.

My task in this chapter is to think with you about how we might approach the difficult moments in church leadership. I would like to suggest five ideas in the form of five short phrases.

THINK LIKE YOU ARE CHINESE

First, when you have a difficult moment, *think like you are Chinese.* For seven years I have been privileged to teach as visiting professor in Hong Kong's City University. I am particularly fascinated with the Chinese language. I could never learn to speak it. I could never learn to write it. But I am fascinated because so much of the language has a message for us. Unpack the Chinese characters that make up the words and you will find pictures. Pictures that communicate. If you look closely at the characters that make up the word "crisis" you will find a message regarding the two ways a difficult moment can be viewed. On one side is a picture of someone standing on a ledge. A sharp dagger-like object points up from the ground below. The Chinese picture essentially says, "Watch out, there could be some danger!" Fall off the ledge on to that sharp object, and it is going to cause harm. In essence, when you have a crisis or difficult moment, there is a dimension of real danger.

The second picture in the word "crisis" is also instructive. It includes the symbols of a tree and a table or workbench. The pictures seek to communicate that a crisis presents both danger and opportunity. You can cut down the tree, and with tools and workbench you can make something of it.

Think about your life for a moment. Consider those situations you can point to and say, "There was a moment I really grew. There was a moment I matured. There was a moment I learned something." I would guess most of those were difficult experiences. Most of those were times of crisis. You look back and say, "I would not want to do it again, but I learned something important and life-changing."

The same is true with difficult situations in the church community. There are dangers *and* wonderful opportunities. If our view of difficult experiences is only to view them as dangerous, we just might miss what God is trying to do among us.

A difficult situation occurred in my ministry several years ago. My home congregation decided to redecorate the inside of our church building. I was heavily involved in that project. We had a great deal of support for doing the construction. But I made a terrible mistake. I believed what the contractors told me about the project's cost and duration. I should never have done that. I have learned my lesson. Regarding the completion date, they said, "For six weeks your church must worship somewhere else. We simply cannot have the scaffolding up and have you running in and out of the auditorium. You can return in six weeks."

We found a place to meet a block down the street—a Jewish temple. Our leadership team thought that it presented an interesting moment and put its very best face on the circumstance for 350 people. We announced the plan and the fact that we would only be gone from our building for about six weeks. We explained that in six weeks we would be back in a newly renovated facility.

As such projects go, we began to realize that six weeks was a little optimistic. So was eight weeks. So was twelve weeks. Then the Jewish Temple folks indicated that they had other commitments for their building. So we went down the street a little farther and met in a junior high school auditorium. Not everyone was excited about it. The danger of dissatisfaction increased. Yet, in the danger was an opportunity, the opportunity to decide if our church was a building or a community. If we defined ourselves as a building, people could get frustrated, upset and perhaps leave our fellowship. But if we defined ourselves as a community of faith, we probably could handle a longer-than-anticipated sojourn. That important question for a congregation would never have been asked if the contractors had been on time. As it turns out, the congregation had marvelous patience, a reaffirmation of its ability to endure disruption, and a clear sense of God's presence.

When faced with difficult moments, think like you are Chinese. Recognize the danger and look for the opportunity. They both may exist in the circumstances you face.

Focus on the Process

My second suggestion is to *focus on the process*. In every difficult moment you can choose where you focus. You can focus on the *substance* or you can focus on the *process*. The substance has to do with the matter that concerns us. What songs should we sing in worship? That is a question of substance. What should our policy be on the use of the church van? That is a substantive question. What is the doctrinal interpretation of a particular passage? That is a question of substance. As a church, we spend a great deal of time on substance, and that is because we have a high view of Scripture. Answers are important. Seeking answers causes us to focus on the substance of the issues.

Substance is very important. At times, however there is a more important focus for a congregation's leaders: focus on the *process*. In other words, the "what" may at times be less important for leaders than the "how."

When I was the Director of the Straus Institute for Dispute Resolution at Pepperdine University School of Law, a colleague coined the phrase "the right answer at the wrong time is the wrong answer." In essence he suggested that I can have the right answer but if I present it at the wrong time, communicate it in the wrong way, or am not sensitive to the context in which it is offered, I probably will not be convincing.

All who understand missions or evangelism understand this. I can have the "right answer" that says you should believe in the Lord Jesus Christ, confess him as Lord and Savior, be baptized, and be added to a congregation of the Lord's people. But if I go down to Kinko's, where I was recently, walk up to the wonderful assistant manager, and tell her that, do you think it is going to be effective? Do you think she's going to say, "I've never thought about that before. I'm ready to go right now!" Or might the assistant manager be a little puzzled that this guy in a blue sweater is preaching to her at ten o'clock in the morning in

Kinko's. It wouldn't make sense in that context. Not because it is the wrong answer, but because it is not the right process. We know that one of the ways people are drawn to faith is through a relationship with the person who teaches them. Effective evangelism is not the result of a guy in a blue sweater showing up and telling a stranger about the right answer.

Effective leaders might conclude that there are real congregational issues to be resolved, but leaders may need to be more focused on *how* to get there than *where* we are going." You may not know exactly where you are going, but you do have the responsibility to manage well getting there.

About twelve years ago leaders in my congregation decided it would be appropriate for women to have a larger role in a number of church activities including worship. But at the same time we said, "While we believe that it would be acceptable, we are not going to do anything until the congregation decides that it is time." Ten years passed and the matter came up again. This time the judgment was to consider the matter anew. But, it was not a matter of saying, "Ten years ago a group of elders decided this, so here we go." Rather, we announced, "Ten years ago a group of elders wrestled with this and we think God is calling us to consider it again. We do not know where it is going, we are not telling you what the result will be, but we invite you to join us on that journey."

Leaders spent several Sunday mornings focused on relevant biblical directions. For several Sunday nights leaders engaged in structured dialogue with hundreds from the congregation. During these weeks elders made themselves available in various ways to work with the congregation. A large number of people participated in the process. In fact, church attendance during these weeks of consideration was the highest in the church's history. The conversation excited people and they wanted to be a part. As changes were made, 98 percent of the members, even some who disagreed with the change, remained a part of that fellowship. Care related to the process as opposed to an obsession with the substance created a positive and peaceful outcome.

GO BELOW THE LINE

My third suggestion in managing difficult moments is to *go below the line*. Conflict is fairly predictable. It begins with the identification of an issue. An issue tends to be measurable and often tangible. Issues set our conversation's agenda. If someone walks in and says, "I have a concern to express to the leadership of this congregation," we know that they are probably going to identify an issue. Typically when an issue is identified, people take a position on that issue. A position is really a perspective. A position essentially says, "Based upon my experience, education, and cultural context, this is how I see it." Someone else often responds, "I feel a little differently about it." Then, we can predict what happens next. One side tries to convince the other side that its perspective is right. The other side responds advocating its perspective and often the conflict escalates. As the conflict escalates the conversation gets more intense and focused on the people, not the problem. And parties are no closer to resolving anything. Our model of resolving conflict is to say, "Tell me what this issue is and I will tell you my position."

Take, for instance, a conflict over the selection of songs for worship. Some want to sing praise songs while others want to sing traditional hymns. Each takes a position to convince the other. No one changes a position. The question becomes, "What is the leadership going to do about the selection of songs for worship?"

The most important four words in all of conflict management might be helpful: *go below the line*. You will see why these words make sense when you have a drawing in your head. On top in the center is the word "issue." To either side are positions. A line is drawn under the positions. Below it is interest information. Interest information causes people to take positions. Interest information drives people, motivates people, and expands the positions they take. If the interest information becomes part of the conversation a creative outcome is more likely. If conversation stays above the line possibilities are limited. Might either party convince the other? Not likely. They may compromise, but many disputes within the middle ground are not satisfactory. One or both of the parties could simply walk away. Those responses are neither helpful nor biblical.

Consider the apostle Paul. Remember that moment in Acts 17 when Paul went into Athens and discovered the idols? Paul could have taken a position on idol worship. After all, Paul knew idols were not gods to be worshipped. He could have started an argument about idol worship. He could have faced off with the Athenians. Paul was wiser than that. What did he do? He said, "As I look around at all those idols I see that you are very religious." An argument would have been above the line. His statement was below the line. He begins the conversation by acknowledging the other side! When was the last time we did that in a church? When was the last time a leader said, "I want us to begin this conversation by recognizing how much we appreciate your passion on this issue. It is obvious that it is important to you. You are invested in who we are and what we do, and we, as your leadership team, applaud that"? Instead, we often say, "Tell me what your position is, and I will decide if I agree or not."

Paul says, "I see you are very religious. And you have erected this idol over here to an unknown god. May I talk for just a few minutes about the unknown God?" Paul brings them into a different kind of conversation and the text records that many that day were brought to believe in that unknown God. He could have argued with them, but instead, he went below the line to the level of their interest in religion and eventually brought some into relationship with God.

Let me share another example of "going below the line" from my professional mediation practice. The case involved a sixty-two-year-old woman who had worked for a large company for thirty years. She never had a bad personnel evaluation but was suddenly terminated with a number of other older women about to retire.

The mediation occurred about six weeks before trial. We started with the woman and lawyers in one room. The conversation quickly went where lawyers live—above the line. What is the issue in the case? The issue is whether or not the corporation is guilty of discrimination. Interesting. What's your position? One side declared that its position is that the company is guilty. The other side disagreed. What a surprise! They have been fighting this out for two years. One side gives all the reasons she is going to win; the other side responds with all the reasons she is going to loose.

Finally it is my turn, as mediator, to intervene and ask a question. With whom do I want to talk? I want to talk to the sixty-two-year-old woman in the room. I want you to picture this. She is sitting in a chair with her legs crossed, her arms crossed, and clinging onto her purse. Now I am not a psychologist, but my sense is that this was not a particularly comfortable moment for her. I knew I should treat her with care. And so I said, "Your lawyers have done an excellent job getting this case prepared for trial but I would like to ask you this one question: What is it that you really want out of the case?" I was prepared for her to say, "I want a million dollars and the company president dead!" I had no idea what she would say.

She was very nervous as she sat there and almost under her breath said, "All I want is what I would have had." So I followed up and asked "What would you have had?" She said, "If they would have just let me work for two more years I could have retired. I could have had medical benefits for the rest of my life. But because they terminated me, I don't get them."

I continued, "Why are your medical benefits so important?" She replied, "If you understood my situation, you would know.

I have worked for this company for thirty years. I have never had a bad evaluation. The best year I had I made $17,000. But it has been very difficult. I'm the sole supporter of my adult son who has polio and have all support responsibilities for my adult daughter with MS. My husband is terminally ill with cancer. I need those medical benefits."

It was absolutely quiet in that room full of lawyers. For the first time they understood what their own case was about. This was a case about a sixty-two-year-old woman who needed medical benefits. That was it.

I sent her out in the lobby so I could work with the lawyers. When she left I shared an observation with the lawyers, "Look. It sounds to me as if we're talking about her medical benefits, and if we just take care of those we might settle the case." One defense lawyer slammed his hand down on the table and said, "Look, if what you're telling me to pay is $287,000 you can forget it!" Whoa. He already had it calculated. Finally one of the lawyers said, "The problem is her status. If she was retired, she would be one of 4,000 in the retiree medical plan. It wouldn't cost much. Because she was terminated, however, she's not eligible for that benefit." Then they got creative.

Two hours later the executive vice president came over from company headquarters. He addressed the woman and made the following offer: "Tomorrow we're giving you a check for last year's wages. We know you've been off work and it has been difficult. We are also going to cover your legal fees. We just worked that out with your lawyers. We also want to do something that may seem a little strange. We want to rehire you for two years, after which you may retire. You will get your medical benefits for the rest of your life. During your two years of employment we will pay you your salary with all benefits. One more thing. If, during the next two years you wish stay home and take care of your family, it's fine with us."

Did the case settle that day? Of course it did. Defense counsel walked down the hall with me and said, "Randy, we think we saved three or four hundred thousand dollars on that case." I walked back in the mediation room. The woman was sitting with her lawyer, crying. She has all she ever had plus something she never imagined: the opportunity to stay home and take care of her family.

Now my question for you: if we can do that in eight hours with a piece of litigation in the secular world, is not there some way we could do the same thing in our communities of faith? The key is: *go below the line.*

USE THE SATISFACTION TRIANGLE

My fourth suggestion is to *use the satisfaction triangle.* When we do the hard work of reconciliation—focusing on the process, listening for people's interests, being creative in our response—how do we know if we have handled the process well? Let me suggest areas of satisfaction in the context of three sides of a triangle.

The first area to examine is the *product,* or outcome, of the response to a difficult moment. Imagine it as the base of a triangle. Is there an outcome to which the people involved can be committed? Not everyone will necessarily love it, but can most people say, "This is a direction we can support"? Satisfaction with regard to the "what" will be critical to future success.

Second, the left side of the triangle has to do with the *process* or, stated another way, the level of processing satisfaction. Were credibility and integrity obtained during resolution? Will the people involved say, "Those folks worked as hard on *how* they did it as on *what* they did"? If so, they may attribute credibility and integrity to the process which are essential in achieving a satisfactory outcome.

Finally, the right side of the triangle has to do with the people and how they believe they were treated. It relates to their psychological satisfaction. Do they feel as if they had a chance to be heard and to participate in the process? Were people validated and affirmed as individuals? Are they satisfied with their feelings as well as the analysis? While difficult to measure, the psychological level of satisfaction is also a critical element.

If you have all three elements of satisfaction, whether it is an elder selection process, a move to a new facility, or a decision about how your congregation is going to worship together, you have led well. If you are missing substantially in any one of those areas, you might want to think about it before you go rushing forward. If people do not support the outcome, do not feel as if the process had credibility, or do not feel as if they were recognized in the process, they will oppose the change. They might not even know why they have such anxiety about it, but their dissatisfaction will be made known. On the other hand, if the process has been characterized as having integrity and credibility and you have treated the people really well, the congregation will be tolerant of outcomes that are not their first choice.

My family's congregation tolerated well the changes and adjustments that came with dynamic ministry. In our nineteen-year experience leadership openly acknowledged that no one member would probably like everything all of the time. Instead, an expectation of tolerance permeated the congregation. It was a refreshing kind of community to be in—one that eliminated tremendous conflict by managing conflict well. People stayed, not because it was perfect or always to their liking, but because difficult moments were handled in ways that honored both people and processes. The satisfaction triangle reminded the congregation's leadership of the elements needed to achieve ongoing commitment to the body.

REMEMBER GOD'S PROMISE

The fifth and last suggestion is *remember God's promise.* Some of the suggestions in this chapter have focused on practical steps anyone can take. This final suggestion reminds us that God has made real promises to us. God promised in the Old Testament that if we as people humble ourselves, ask for forgiveness, and turn from our wicked ways then God would heal us. That is a promise. It is a promise with some order to it. There is a requirement for us to say, "Take us God, humble us and turn us from things we should not be doing. Make us the kind of people you want us to be." Behind that requirement is a promise that God will heal our lives and heal our churches. In the difficult moments God is still with us. God wants our churches to be vibrant, exciting communities for his service.

I close with the story of an African-American Baptist church in a large eastern city. The church had a conflict. If you attended on a Sunday when conflict enveloped the church, you would have felt it. The argument was about whether or not the church should build a new building. The pastor had received a death threat. "If you ever preach in this church again, it'll be the last sermon you ever preach." The next Sunday on the podium next to him were two bodyguards. The preacher looked out on his congregation, felt the discomfort of the bulletproof vest underneath his white starched shirt. The tension was palpable. The conflict grew worse, and according to Baptist tradition, a vote was scheduled to determine if the pastor should stay or go. The debate raged. People expressed different views. The conflict was loud, bitter, and divisive. Hundreds of people gathered at the church building to vote.

Over in the corner a frail, elderly, black woman looked over the scene. This was not the church she knew. These people were not acting like her people. She had no idea what to do. She had no office. She had no power. What could she do to stop this mob scene? She did the only thing she could think to do. With her timid voice she began to sing. A simple confessional song, "If I have wounded any soul today, if I have caused one foot to go astray, if I have walked in my own willful way, dear Lord, forgive." What would you do, standing next to her? What would you do by the side of one carrying out the ministry of reconciliation? Soon others began to sing. Soon the song caught on and there emerged a very different moment in that Baptist church.

They did not take a vote that afternoon. Several years later, early on a Sunday morning, my son and I worshipped at that church. In the new church building hundreds of people were continuing God's work. It took a frail, elderly woman to remind that large congregation of God's promise. The confession in song led to God's healing. In the intensity of difficult moments, remember God's promises.

For nineteen years as Director of The Straus Institute for Dispute Resolution at Pepperdine University School of Law, I closed one training program with these words: "Peace is not the absence of conflict. Peace is that state when conflict is managed effectively, efficiently and respectfully." We will never live in a world without difficult moments, but we can learn to handle them in a way that brings peace to those relationships we value. Blessed are the peacemakers.

BIBLIOGRAPHY

Bridges, William. *Managing Transitions.* Cambridge, MA: Perseus Books, 1991.

Cosgrove, Charles H. and Dennis D. Hatfield. *Church Conflict: The Hidden Systems Behind the Fights.* Nashville, TN: Abingdon, 1994.

Halverstadt, Hugh F. *Managing Church Conflict.* Louisville, KY: Westminster/John Knox, 1991.

Hicks, H. Beecher, Jr. *Preaching Through a Storm.* Grand Rapids, MI: Zondervan, 1987.

Lott, David B., Editor. *Conflict Management in Congregations.* Bethesda, MD: Alban Institute, 2001.

Sande, Ken. *Managing Conflict in Your Church.* Billings, MT: Institute for Christian Conciliation, 1993.

Sande, Ken. *The Peacemaker.* Grand Rapids, MI: Baker, 1991.

Susek, Ron. *Firestorm: Preventing and Overcoming Church Conflicts.* Grand Rapids, MI: Baker, 1999.

Chapter 7

THE CHURCH GOES TO THE MOVIES

Standing at the Intersection of Christianity and Popular Culture

Greg Stevenson

Parents and church leaders often look at the popular culture around them and shudder in fear at its negative impact upon younger generations. But is this anything new? Consider the following quotation: "Even the perversion of music has increased today, and extravagances in clothes and foot-wear have reached a climax."[1] That sentiment comes from the Greek author Athenaeus, writing around AD 200. Over 1,800 years ago, Athenaeus surveyed the youth culture of his day and concluded that it had gotten as bad as it could get. But, we protest, today television and film have brought us untold degradations that certainly make the current generation unique in its pursuit of the unholy. No doubt film and television have added some new wrinkles, but the clothing is the same. The book *Our Movie Made Children* laments the effect of film on the youth of society: "There is probably something socially wrong, something subversive of the best interests of society in the way a substantial number of present-day movies are made, written, conceived....The road to delinquency, in a few words, is heavily dotted with movie addicts."[2] Many of us would likely add a hearty "Amen" to that. The problem? That statement was published in 1933. This was the decade that gave us Jimmy Stewart! Yet many adults of that era looked at the product coming out of Hollywood and saw only the dissolution of our morals and values.

My point is simply this: the contemporary battle in our culture and in our churches over the impact that mainstream entertainment has on the moral fabric of society is nothing new. The older generations have always cast a suspicious eye on the entertainment choices of the young. This trend goes back at least as far as Plato who believed that popular culture was corrupting youth and who thus advocated censorship and wanted to ban the mass entertainment of his day—poetry readings of Homer and the theater. In the early days of Christianity, church leaders like Origen and Augustine attacked the corrupting influence of the theater. We could trace the evolution of these cultural battles throughout history: Shakespeare, the Davy Crockett almanacs of the nineteenth century, the early American theater and vaudeville, the radio programs of the 1930's, and then, of course, there is always Elvis.

The present-day conflict between the church and Holly-wood is ancestor to a long and vibrant tradition. It is an ancient beast that we have been fighting a long time. Yet, it is also an ancient beast that has gotten itself some new teeth.

CHURCH, TECHNOLOGY, AND YOUTH IN THE TWENTY-FIRST CENTURY

The twenty-first century is producing some unique challenges for the church. Unprecedented technological change is causing our culture to evolve at a rate unlike any before. The challenge is whether the church can keep pace as technological innovation presents us with situations we never dreamt of before. Cloning, stem cell research, gene manipulation, and Internet pornography are issues unimagined by our biblical authors. Church members are having extra-marital affairs not in motel rooms, but in chat rooms. We find ourselves having to navigate uncharted waters in trying to communicate the biblical message to a culture very different from those in which the Bible was written.

While America's youth are embracing technological innovation with a rabid fervor, the church as a whole is often uncomfortable with such advancement because it frequently calls for change. This increases the generation gap between young and old in the church as younger believers increasingly view the "old guard" of the church as being hopelessly out of touch with the culture. Consequently, many churches across America struggle to attract younger individuals. This is a problem that goes beyond traditional debates over doctrine and rituals. It is a universal problem that cuts across geographical and denominational (and non-denominational) lines.

In a nutshell, the problem is that many younger believers are rejecting organized religion. Note that this trend does not constitute a rejection of God as such but only a rejection of the church. Numerous studies have demonstrated a growing tendency in American culture for individuals to embrace spirituality while rejecting religion. One study of college students indicated that 70 percent of the students surveyed believe that people can grow spiritually without being religious. Among this same group, 77 percent prayed regularly but only 20 percent of those claimed any serious religious involvement, such as attending worship services.[3] Essentially people are seeking God today; they are just concluding that the church is not the place to find him. When many look at the church, they see an institution that defines itself in terms of decades-old debates over doctrines and practices rather than defining itself in terms of the heart of the gospel message: love God and love each other.

Obviously this is a multi-faceted problem that involves numerous components—most of which this essay does not address. My concern is to focus upon only one small aspect of the problem; that is, how the church's traditional approach to film and television contributes to the disconnect between the leaders of churches and their younger members.

The challenge to church leaders is this: how does the church communicate its relevance to the younger generations in a twenty-first-century, media-saturated culture? The theological foundation for answering that question comes from Hebrews 4:11-12a: "Let us therefore make every effort to enter that rest, so that no one may fall through such disobedience as theirs. Indeed, the word of God is living and active."[4] This author quotes from Psalm 95 and offers an extended interpretation of its meaning for his audience. He concludes in 4:11 by exhorting his audience to enter the rest spoken of in the psalm. He thus takes a psalm written hundreds of years earlier to a different audience and in a very different culture and claims that it speaks to his present time. How can he do that? Psalm 95 was not written in his time or within his culture. He gives his justification for doing this in the next verse: "the word of God is living and active."

To say that Scripture is alive and active is to say that it continually adapts itself to new times and new cultures. This is why we can take writings that are 2,000/3,000 years removed from us and confidently claim that they speak to us. The word of God is inherently designed to adapt to every new situation and culture. One responsibility of the church is to allow the word of God to do what it is designed to do without getting in its way. The gospel message does not change, but how we communicate that message and how we adapt that message to the culture must change as the culture changes or else we become the impediment to communication. Even though the gospel message is active and alive, we have often treated it as though it is stationary and stagnant. How else to explain that we live in a media-saturated culture, and yet we continue to employ methods of evangelism, worship styles, and cultural attitudes more at home in the 1960's?

How should the church respond to the challenges of a twenty-first-century culture? How do we adapt with the culture, while not adapting to the culture? In particular, how does the church adapt to a media-saturated culture in a way that communicates the church's relevance in that culture, while avoiding association with the often immoral messages that thrive in that culture?

Historically, the church does not have a good track record in its relationship with Hollywood. Christians have correctly sought to be a prophetic voice challenging the culture rather than one conforming to the culture. The solution is not for the church to become more like Hollywood. Going to church should never be on par with going to the movie theater. Christians absolutely must take a stand on issues of morality and strive to live lives of holiness in all aspects of the culture. Nevertheless, in our desire to accomplish this, we have traditionally adopted a stance towards the entertainment industry that, more often than not, fails to achieve the goals we seek. This stance derives in part from a belief that the church and Hollywood are in competition with one another. How often have we lamented the fact that younger Christians spend more time watching TV than reading the Bible, that they spend more money on DVD's and CD's than they give to the church, and that their values and beliefs are often shaped more by the media than by the pulpit? We acknowledge that we stand in competition with Hollywood for the time, wallets, and values of the people in our communities. Because we see ourselves battling with Hollywood over the same territory, we thus conclude that we are at *war*. And if we are at war, then Hollywood must be the enemy. Consequently, we barricade ourselves behind the walls of the church and lob out verbal grenades at the entertainment industry. We boycott advertisers of programs we don't like in an attempt to hurt their bottom line, much like an army seeking to take out an enemy's economic infrastructure. We demonize Hollywood and align it with Satan.

Although the entertainment industry is certainly not without responsibility for the negative moral influence it has had on society, the results of our years of attack have not had their desired impact. Rather than seeing younger believers turn their backs on the entertainment industry and repudiate its products, we have seen them more commonly turn their backs on the church. This is not because they accept everything that comes out of Hollywood and thus make a conscious choice to embrace immorality over morality. Rather, it is because they see the church as an institution that has failed to comprehend the important role entertainment media plays in their lives and, even more devastating, has shown little interest in doing so. This is a critical point because if younger believers perceive the church as being incapable of understanding twenty-first-century culture, then they may also see it as incapable of showing people how to find God in that culture.

Many parents and church leaders have not come to grips with the role of the entertainment media today because they continue to operate with three fundamental misconceptions. They misconceive the nature of film and television, the function of film and television in American culture, and the nature of media morality.

MISCONCEPTION #1: THE NATURE OF FILM AND TELEVISION

The Detroit News interviewed a sixty-eight-year-old woman about her reaction to the 2004 Superbowl half-time debacle starring Janet Jackson's infamous "wardrobe malfunction." She responded, "Last year's Super Bowl halftime was like a lot of things on TV—disgusting. If I had young children today, I wouldn't let them watch TV."[5] Her response represents the common assumption that television is inherently immoral and designed for the sole purpose of corrupting societal values. Television corrupts and thus the only proper response for those who care about values and morality is to get rid of their televisions. This viewpoint manifests in the form of Christians who proudly announce to all who will listen that they have banned television in their household—as though that were a badge of virtue. This viewpoint, however, stems from the fundamental misunderstanding that television and film is somehow inherently evil.

The fact is that television and film are morally *neutral*. They are nothing more than a means of communication just as literature is a means of communication. The bias against television derives in part from a bias against visual communication. Many operate with the assumption that seeing a story is inherently less beneficial and more capable of corruption than reading a story. One could walk into any bookstore today and find countless volumes that contain sex, violence, and profanity, promote false philosophies, and communicate dangerous ideas. Yet we do not advocate getting rid of books. Television critic David Bianculli suggests that having a national "Turn off the TV Day" makes as much sense as having a national "Don't Pick Up a Book Day." Responding to Jerry Mander's dictate, "I never watch TV, and neither should you," Bianculli replies: "It's the video equivalent of an illiterate proudly proclaiming, 'I never read books or newspapers, and neither should you.' Dismissing television in its entirety makes no more sense than dismissing the printing press."[6] Bianculli's point is that the medium itself is not the problem. Yes, much of what can be found on television is immoral, but the same is true for what can be found in any bookstore. The medium is morally neutral, but how that medium is used determines its moral value.

Accepting the moral neutrality of television and film means acknowledging that moral evaluation must proceed in terms of the assessment of individual programs and not of the medium as a whole. It means acknowledging that just as there is much on television that is harmful and morally degrading, there is also much that is morally inspiring, educationally beneficial, artistically moving, and intellectually stimulating. Earlier we discussed the trend of people rejecting organized religion, while embracing God and spirituality. As unfortunate as this trend may be, it has given rise to a theological conversation that is occurring in our culture outside of the walls of the church, and television and film have become one of the primary arenas in which this conversation unfolds. Television, in particular, provides a forum for the communication of moral and spiritual issues, often in profound ways. The first season finale of *Joan of Arcadia* functioned as a visual depiction of biblical lament that was more theologically profound and spiritually moving than any sermon I have heard on the topic. That it was presented visually in the form of a story reveals the power of television. While I have forgotten far too many Sunday sermons, the visual presentation of lament in this one *Joan of Arcadia* episode has stayed with me for a year as I continue to revisit it and process its message.

The dark secret that many in the church want to ignore is that, like it or not, the younger generations in this country are engaged in this conversation. They are getting theology. They are just getting it from the television and not from the church. Unfortunately, we Christians have become so suspicious of Hollywood as a rule that we have largely chosen to opt out of this conversation. We prefer to complain and point fingers at the people who are out there in the culture generating spiritual discussion instead of choosing to add our voice to that conversation. If the church is to communicate its relevance in a media-saturated culture, it must adopt a more balanced attitude toward television and film. The church certainly cannot ignore what is bad or immoral, but it should also be willing to embrace what is good and even to recognize that good and bad frequently coexist within the same film or show. The church should be willing and able to become a part of the cultural conversation, not in a finger-pointing way, but in a way that engages people in honest and constructive dialogue over what they see and watch.

The church has an important and essential voice to add to this conversation. That people are seeking spirituality even outside the walls of the church is actually good news because it provides a starting point for dialogue. Our willingness to interact openly and constructively with the entertainment media and with those who watch it extends Paul's Athenian model. By discussing poetry about Zeus with Stoic and Epicurean philosophers, Paul was joining the theological conversation of his day and adding the church's voice to it.

Any constructive dialogue is a two-way street. If we actively engage the theological conversation generated by and through film and television, we may be surprised to discover that not only can we bring a vital perspective to bear, but we also can learn something from that conversation as well.

MISCONCEPTION #2: THE FUNCTION OF TELEVISION
AND FILM IN AMERICAN YOUTH CULTURE

Film and television play many roles in American culture, but by far the most popular conception of their function is that they are "just entertainment." This deep-seated belief that popular media exist only to excite us and provide pleasure has affected the attitudes of many adults in the church towards youth. We see young people "wasting their time" watching TV or movies instead of being engaged in more noble pursuits like reading the New Testament or studying church history. Consequently, we conclude that our youth are so conditioned by an entertainment-obsessed culture that they want worship to entertain them as well.

This perception may bear some truth, but ultimately it operates with a fundamental misconception about the function of film and television within youth culture. Although film and television are entertainment, nothing could be further from the truth than the claim that they are *just* entertainment. America's youth today have inherited a media-saturated culture pervaded by film, television, music, video games, and the Internet. This is the only world they have known and they are fully conditioned by it. It affects how they learn, how they think, and how they relate to the world around them. They are trained by the culture to learn visually as opposed to the traditional format of lecture or sermon. To put it bluntly, visual media is a fundamental component of their *language*. Thus, it is not surprising that churches are not communicating well with younger people because these churches are not speaking their language. There is a reason why a young person can sit riveted for two hours watching "The Passion of the Christ" and come away emotionally moved and intellectually stimulated and yet that same person struggles mightily to stay awake for a twenty-minute sermon on the cross. Very few people would argue that the reason is because "The Passion of the Christ" was entertaining. The film connects more powerfully with them not because of some inherent entertainment value, but because it speaks to them in their language. If church leaders today do not come to grips with the fact that there is a significant language barrier between the older and younger generations in our culture, then they will fail to communicate the gospel message as effectively as possible within this culture.

When talking about the language of youth, one must speak of story. One reason Hollywood often communicates more effectively with our youth than does the church is because film and television speak the language of story, while church members are oddly uncomfortable with this language. Stories are a subtle form of communication that employ metaphors and symbols, thus leaving it up to the hearer (or viewer) to put the pieces together. This is unnerving to many church members because if we try to communicate our message through story, then we risk having our audience put the pieces together in a way we did not intend. We are fearful that if we speak in story and metaphor, then the gospel might be misunderstood. Ironically, Jesus did not share this concern or else he would not have spoken so often in parables. The Bible itself is essentially a story from beginning to end. Yet instead of embracing this primary language of Scripture, we cling tenaciously to neat, straightforward propositions and sermons that state clearly what we should or should not do and believe. This lust for unambiguous propositions has led us to take the biblical story of salvation and turn it into laundry lists of steps to follow and moral do's and don'ts. The fact that God chose to reveal himself to us primarily through story should tell us that we lose something very valuable when we neglect this form of communication.

For twenty-first-century youth, stories are an essential means of connecting to the world around them. A culture's stories are what create identity and shape its values and beliefs. Stories help to explain the world and teach us how to live in it. Is it any wonder that God revealed himself through stories? Stories are much less about entertainment than they are about meaning. In particular, stories function for youth as "maps of reality." These stories teach them how to navigate the often confusing worlds of adolescence and adulthood by charting "meanings, values, assumptions, attitudes, behavioral norms, and social and gender roles."[7] And the primary generators of stories in our culture today are film and television.

How can the church respond to this language and culture barrier? Although many valid responses are available, I will highlight two suggestions that provide a good beginning point.

Suggestion #1: Take television and film seriously. Church leaders need to break out of the confining view of popular media as being "just entertainment" and acknowledge it as a significant purveyor of meaning in our culture, both for good and for ill. Academics have been paving the way in this regard. While engendering much ridicule from those who fail to comprehend the cultural impact and importance of television, academics have been busy analyzing the "maps of reality" provided by shows such as *Star Trek, The Simpsons,* and *The X-Files.*

Surpassing them all has been *Buffy the Vampire Slayer.* Numerous doctoral dissertations from the United States, Australia, and the United Kingdom have been and are being produced on this show. Scholarly journal publications on *Buffy the Vampire Slayer* have come out of virtually every academic field.

In addition to academics, the creators of film and television recognize the cultural value of their work and its role in providing meaning and guidance to youth. Responding to the academic interest in his show, Joss Whedon, the creator of *Buffy the Vampire Slayer*, says:

> I think it's great that the academic community has taken an interest in the show. I think it's always important for academics to study popular culture....We think very carefully about what we're trying to say emotionally, politically, and even philosophically while we're writing....People used to laugh that academics would study Disney movies. There's nothing more important for academics to study, because [we] shape the minds of our children....[8]

Likewise, George Lucas, creator of *Star Wars,* comments on the cultural importance of film.

> Film and visual entertainment are a pervasively important part of our culture, an extremely significant influence on the way our society operates. People in the film industry don't want to accept the responsibility that they had a hand in the way the world is loused up. But, for better or worse, the influence of the church, which used to be all-powerful, has been usurped by film. Films and television tell us the way we conduct our lives, what is right and wrong. It's important that the people who make films have ethics classes, philosophy classes, history classes. Otherwise, we're witch doctors.[9]

Lucas' observation that film has usurped the cultural influence of the church, whether correct or not, is an observation that the church has failed to learn how to speak the language of the culture and, thus, people are turning to film and television to find stories that give meaning to life. Note that this desire for meaningful stories may not be a conscious one. The stories in our culture provide maps of reality regardless of whether the hearers or viewers recognize them as such. Many are attracted to the stories in the popular media without fully understanding that attraction.

Whereas academics and artists recognize the cultural role that visual stories play in American youth culture, church leaders and many parents have been comparatively slow in recognizing this phenomenon, thus unknowingly increasing the generation gap between them and the young. The most important element here is communication. When parents or church leaders simply attack the movies or shows that younger people watch, what those young people take away is that their feelings are not respected and that what matters to them is not taken seriously. A d u l t s must understand that the movies, television shows, and music of their children is not "just entertainment," but is one of the means by which they connect to, cope with, and make sense of the world around them. This understanding on the part of adults is particularly vital because their children and teenagers may not be aware of how these stories impact them. All they know is that this media speaks to them. Consequently, the first step for parents and church leaders is to listen to their children and to their younger church members. Recognize that what youth see in a television show or movie is often not what their parents see. It is important for parents to ask their children why they like the shows or the music they do and, if they will answer, to take those answers seriously. This does not mean that parents give the rubber stamp of approval to everything their children see or hear. Rather, it means that even when needing to caution against a show or to forbid the hearing of a particular song, it should be done in a way that represents understanding and appreciation for what these forms of communication mean to them.

Suggestion #2: Learn to speak their language. Many churches realize the need to engage the entertainment media in some way as a means of reaching youth. However, the common solution often takes the form of a "contemporary worship style." This stems in part from the assumption that if we can just be more like the culture and more like Hollywood, just without the immorality, then we can attract them. The unofficial motto seems to be: "If we turn on the DVD player, they will come." So we institute praise teams, updated music, videos and drama in the belief that what people are searching for is simply a contemporary *form* of worship. This is the myth of the contemporary worship style and it is a potentially poisonous belief to the spiritual health of our churches. We desire simple fixes and would like to slap on some spiritual Neosporin and a Band-Aid and make the problem go away. So we focus on the form of worship because that is something we can easily correct. But the reality is far more complex and much less easily resolved.

Because more progressive churches are fairly consistent in their proclamation that a contemporary worship style is the answer to the generation gap, I had assumed they were on to something—until I had opportunity to study the issue myself. Studies and research informed me that contemporary worship was not primarily what the younger generations were seeking. This ran counter to the message I was hearing from church leaders, so I was skeptical. Consequently, I decided to adopt a personal approach. I conducted an unofficial survey among fifty sophomores, juniors and seniors in my classes at Rochester College. I asked a variety of questions relating to what they were most looking for in a church and what would most attract them to worship at a particular congregation. The results surprised me. Only five percent of the students claimed that a contemporary worship style (praise teams, drama, video use, etc) was what they most sought in a church. Wondering if those results were a fluke, I tried the survey again with a class of fifty freshmen. The number of freshmen primarily seeking a contemporary worship style was eight percent.

Current scholarly research and my own admittedly unprofessional survey pointed to the same conclusion. It is true that young people do not want to be bored in church, but neither are they looking to be entertained. When I talk to my students about the perception that they want to be entertained in church, they typically find that perception insulting and patronizing. Above all, what they want is to be *engaged*. They desire a church that is authentic in its Christian identity. They want a church that, instead of arguing over doctrines or obsessing over rituals, focuses all its attention on Christ and on living out the gospel mandate to love one another and care for the poor. In short, they want a church that actually lives up to being the body of Christ in the world.

Doing that, of course, is not easy. It is much simpler to deceive ourselves into thinking that video clips and praise teams will solve the problem. Certainly offering worship that is contemporary with the culture is important, but too often it ignores the real problem. Many younger Christians believe that churches have become so blinded by obsessive focus on doctrines and practices that they have ignored the heart of the gospel: unity, love for one another, and a passion for social justice in all of its forms—and they are beginning to hold us accountable for that oversight. Consequently, if churches are serious about connecting with youth, their focus ought to be less on style and more on embodying the heart of the gospel. If churches have that, the young people will come regardless of the worship style.

Although drama productions and video clips are not the solution to the generation gap, it is nonetheless vital that the church learn to speak the language of this culture. We must reclaim the value of story. I use the word "reclaim" because story is the language of Scripture. Being faithful to Scripture includes embracing the language through which it speaks. This involves becoming more comfortable with metaphor, subtlety, and indirection than we have typically been. The church ought to be the place where people find the stories that give life meaning and direction; yet, Christians themselves have often formed the barrier to this communication because they have not fully engaged the power of story.

When churches have recognized the need for communicating in the language of the culture, it often manifests in the form of film clips shown during worship or as part of a devotional. Although representing an admirable desire to enter into the culture's theological conversation, such attempts are often poorly handled and frequently counterproductive. The film clip usually functions as little more than an illustration designed to keep people's attention. What is needed is a form of interaction with the stories of our culture in a way that engages them theologically. Many churches are coming up with creative means of doing so, such as the church that held a weekly viewing of each of the five films nominated for a Best Picture Oscar for that year. Then they engaged in discussion over the merits and demerits of each film in terms of its theological and cultural message. Small groups can be a particularly effective way of engaging film or television in dialogue as the group can watch a film or television episode together and then allow a theological discussion to flow out of that. Note that these approaches are not designed as a replacement for Scripture, but rather as an entry point into it. For instance, a small group could watch the movie "Groundhog Day" in which Bill Murray searches for meaning in life and then use that as a foundation for exploring Ecclesiastes.

In addition to direct engagement with film or television, however, there are other ways in which the power of stories can be harnessed for the service of the church. What researchers have shown, and my own survey bore out, was that one of the things young people are seeking in a church (and my freshmen put this #1) is a place where the tough questions of faith can be addressed honestly and openly. One of the most valuable ways to accomplish this is through story. In Rochester College's daily assembly program, students occasionally have an opportunity to give their personal testimonies. Many of our faculty do not see the importance of this practice, preferring instead a biblical lecture or worship-oriented service. To the students, however, these testimonies are vitally important. To them, this is what church should be—a community in which people share their stories. My students tell me that it is through these stories that they learn about one another and that they are not alone in their struggles with life and faith. They learn that they are a part of a community of believers who are all trying to live out the call of Christ.

By contrast, how often in churches do we sit next to people for years and yet know virtually nothing about them? I wonder if the use of personal testimony could even help to bridge the generation gap in the church. What would happen if older members of the congregation got up and told their stories-the stories of their conversion or of difficult times they've faced in relationships or with their faith? What would happen if teenagers got up and spoke about their journey of faith and the challenges that teen culture places before them? One result might be greater mutual understanding and an appreciation that even though separated by many years and by differing cultural factors, we all, young and old alike, are in this together and are all seeking to be encountered by God. Stories make this possible.

MISCONCEPTION #3: THE NATURE OF MEDIA MORALITY

One would assume that Christians, who spend so much time thinking, talking, and reading in Scripture about morality, would be the most adept at evaluating the moral visions of movies and television programs. Yet, the reality is that Christians have been the most simplistic in that endeavor. Enslaved to an obsessive focus on surface content, our standard of moral evaluation typically involves nothing more than tallying instances of sex, violence, and profanity. Certainly these need to be components of any moral evaluation, but when they consist of the entirety of that evaluation, we are operating with a fundamental misunderstanding of how the visual media communicate morality. In fact, the restriction of moral evaluation to instances of sex, violence, and profanity creates two problems.

The first problem with evaluating media solely on the basis of sex, violence, and profanity is that it distorts and limits what is considered moral or immoral. It leads us to fits of rage over a provocative sex scene on primetime all the while leaving us completely unconcerned about overt displays of racism, materialism, cultural idolatry, or the lack of social justice. In the gospels, Jesus spoke more often against the immorality of materialism than he did about sex and violence combined; and yet, we ignore the one and obsess over the other. Our simplistic approach to morality leads us often to condemn a show for a sex scene despite its otherwise healthy message, while praising a show that is devoid of sex, violence, and profanity, but may be immoral in other ways. We will quickly shut off the TV if a woman pops up in a skimpy outfit, but then gather the entire family around to watch *Who Wants to Be a Millionaire.* *Who Wants to Be a Millionaire* is a show with pristine content, but whose overall moral vision centers on greed and materialism. It panders to our lust for wealth and leads us to fantasize about what we would do with all that money. It reinforces the very materialistic urges that Jesus warned us against and is all the more dangerous because of its subtlety.

Likewise, the show *American Idol* was recently hailed by The Parents Television Council as one of the ten best shows of the year in terms of moral content. Their basis for evaluation was simply that it lacked sex, violence, and profanity. That conclusion is logical if our sole standard for evaluation is content. If, however, we include in our evaluation a show's underlying worldview, then we might be led to a different conclusion because *American Idol* represents nothing if not the American deification of fame. Consider how we as a society conceive of actors and musicians. We use the language of deification to describe them when we call them "stars" and "idols." We hang up images of them (posters, billboards) and worship at the altar of celebrity. We exempt them from human standards of morality when we allow them to get away with behavior that we would never condone from other mortals. When we encounter them in person, we stand in awe of their presence. Recently, *US* magazine carried a feature titled "Stars…They're Just Like Us." In it they provide photographs of movie stars engaging in normal human behavior like pumping gas or grocery shopping. The very reason that a magazine has to remind us that stars are just like us is because deep down we wonder if it is true. In this context, a show like *American Idol* reinforces the common belief in America that if you are not famous, you are nobody. Contestants on the show frequently speak in interviews about how desperately they want to be famous and some have even commented after being kicked off that their lives were now over. When someone's identity and self-worth is so tied up in the lust for fame, it is nothing short of cultural idolatry.

The second problem with restricting morality to sex, violence, and profanity is that it ignores the complexity of genuine moral discussion. The issues at play in moral evaluation are far more complex than questions of content. When *The Simpsons* first aired, it came under fierce attack from many Christians and was even publicly condemned by Bill Bennett. Yet, both *Christianity Today* and *The Christian Century* have deemed it one of the most positively religious shows on television.[10] Likewise, *Buffy the Vampire Slayer* has received criticism for its moral content by

Christians and moral watchdog groups like The Parents Television Council. Nevertheless, *National Review* and *Christianity Today* have labeled it one of the most morally serious and religious shows on television.[11] *The Door Magazine* even went so far as to once name Buffy its "Theologian of the Year."[12]

What's going on here? How can two shows create such widely divergent opinions about the state of their morality? The dichotomy represented by these responses demonstrates that the moral evaluation of film and television is a complex endeavor involving numerous factors. But we should already know this from Scripture. Brian Godawa in his book *Hollywood Worldviews* offers an appendix under the title "Sex, Violence & Profanity in the Bible,"[13] in which he raises the question of whether the portrayal of sex, violence, and profanity in the Bible makes the Bible immoral. Of course, the answer is "no," but it leads to the more interesting question of why we then immediately tend to assume that the portrayal of sex, violence, and profanity in film and television necessarily makes them immoral. If the book of Judges were to be faithfully rendered on film today, it would certainly garner no less than an NC-17 rating. Many of the parables of Jesus are full of violent imagery. The Song of Solomon is more sexually explicit, particularly in Hebrew, than many shows on primetime. The story of the crucifixion is mind-numbingly violent, as illustrated by *The Passion of the Christ*. Yet, we do not judge those stories as immoral because we recognize that immoral acts can be portrayed for moral reasons and in moral ways. If we are to approach the subject of morality in film and television with integrity, then we must acknowledge that the same may be true there as well.

This calls for a more sophisticated and nuanced approach to morality than we Christians have often employed. If we think beyond the boundaries of content then we might recognize that issues of context, intent, function, manner of communication, and worldview are equally important factors in moral evaluation.

Exploration of these factors involved in moral evaluation is beyond the scope of this essay (although some of the resources included in the accompanying bibliography can help lead in this direction), but if we can come to see the necessity for engaging media morality in the broader context that it demands, then we have found a vital starting point.

CONCLUDING OBSERVATIONS

Because the media is such a complex entity and it operates within a culture that is constantly in flux, this essay focuses more on diagnosing the illness than treating it. There is no single solution to how the church can best engage the entertainment industry. Every congregation is different and what is appropriate for one may not be for another. The responsibility for deciding how a particular congregation responds to the challenges of our culture rests with its leaders. What is clear is the necessity for Christians to take these challenges seriously. The gospel message is a constant, but the culture in which we proclaim that message never stands still. The Word of God is living and active, constantly on the move and adapting to every time and place. If the church is to be the vehicle through which that Word speaks, it must be willing to move along with it. German theologian Dietrich Bonhoeffer, writing from a Nazi prison, envisioned the day when the church would do just that.

All Christian thinking, speaking, and organizing must be born anew out of this prayer and action....It is not for us to prophesy the day (though the day will come) when men will once more be called so to utter the word of God that the world will be changed and renewed by it. It will be a new language, perhaps quite non-religious, but liberating and redeeming-as was Jesus' language; it will shock people and yet overcome them by its power.[14]

NOTES

1. Athenaeus, Deipnosophists 1.18e.
2. Quoted in David Bianculli, *Teleliteracy: Taking Television Seriously* (Syracuse University Press, 2000), 37-38.
3. *USA Today* (July 28, 2004).
4. Italics added for emphasis.
5. Mekeisha Madden, "TV Decency Debate Tests America's Moral Limits" *The Detroit News and Free Press* (January 16, 2005): 10A.
6. Bianculli, 64.
7. Quentin J. Schultze et al, *Dancing in the Dark: Youth, Popular Culture and the Electronic Media* (Grand Rapids: Eerdmans, 1991), 99.
8. Joss Whedon, interview, *New York Times* (May 16, 2003): Q.1.
9. Quoted in *Dancing in the Dark*, 109-110.
10. John Dart, "Simpsons Have Soul: TV's Most Religious Family?" *Christian Century* 118 (January 2001): 12-14; Mark Pinsky, "Saint Flanders: He's the Evangelical Next Door on *The Simpsons*, and that's Okily Dokily among Many Believers" *Christianity Today* 45 (February 2001): 28-34.
11. Chandler Rosenberger, "Morality Tale…From the Crypt," *National Review* Online (May 26-28, 2001). http://www.nationalreview.com/weekend/television/television-rosenberger052601.shtml.
12. Skippy R., "The Door Theologian of the Year" *The Door Magazine* (Sept./Oct. 2002). http://www.thedoormagazine.com/archives/buffy.html.
13. Brian Godawa, *Hollywood Worldviews: Watching Films with Wisdom and Discernment* (Downers Grove, IL: InterVarsity, 2002), 187-208.
14. Dietrich Bonhoeffer, *Letters and Papers from Prison* (New York: Macmillan, 1972), 300.

BIBLIOGRAPHY

Bianculli, David. *Teleliteracy: Taking Television Seriously.* Syracuse, NY: Syracuse University Press, 2000. Bianculli argues for the cultural and intellectual value of television. The term "teleliteracy" refers to "fluency in the language and content of TV" and Bianculli maintains that this is rapidly becoming the standard for cultural literacy in our culture. He maintains that television is a serious (and potentially beneficial) force in our culture that deserves more respect and academic attention than it has traditionally garnered.

Frost, Michael. *Seeing God in the Ordinary: A Theology of the Everyday.* Hendrickson, 2000. Easy to read and aimed at a popular audience, this book encourages Christians to open their eyes to the presence of God in all aspects of life, particularly contemporary popular culture (film, narrative literature, poetry, etc.). Frost exalts the place of the imagination in Christian life and calls for a renewed Christian interest in story, metaphor, and poetry.

Godawa, Brian. *Hollywood Worldviews: Watching Films with Wisdom and Discernment.* Downer's Grove, IL: InterVarsity, 2002. Written by an award-winning Hollywood screenwriter, this book explores how Christians can benefit from viewing films while protecting their faith from damaging cultural messages. Godawa examines how both philosophical and Christian worldviews find expression through film. This book contains helpful exercises at the end of each chapter designed for use in small groups that seek to explore the intersection of faith and film. Particularly interesting and controversial is an appendix titled "Sex, Violence & Profanity in the Bible."

Johnston, Robert K. *Reel Spirituality: Theology and Film in Dialogue.* Grand Rapids, MI: Baker, 2000. Reel Spirituality is written on more of an academic level than many of the other books on this list, yet the extra perseverance in reading pays off. This is a reasoned examination of the value of film as a means of theological communication.

Jones, Gerard. *Killing Monsters: Why Children NEED Fantasy, Super-Heroes, and Make-Believe Violence.* New York: Basic Books, 2002. A controversial book when it was released, *Killing Monsters* offers a divergent voice to the cacophony of attacks on media violence. He argues that most of the studies claiming that media and fantasy violence promote real violence actually prove the opposite. Jones presents the thesis that a healthy relationship to fantasy violence is actually valuable for the proper development of children by providing them a means of dealing with real-world violence and of learning to gain control over their lives. Jones is a former comic-book and screenwriter who performs Art and Story Workshops for children and adolescents and is the founder of Media Power for Children.

Postman, Neil. *Amusing Ourselves to Death: Public Discourse in the Age of Show Business.* New York: Penguin Books, 1985. For a balancing perspective, Postman argues that television has altered our ability as a culture to tolerate extended public discourse. He suggests we must better understand how the media shapes us if we are to understand how we can best use the media. Postman offers a provocative argument, although it is now somewhat dated.

Romanowski, William D. *Eyes Wide Open: Looking for God in Popular Culture.* Chicago, IL: Brazos, 2001. Romanowski acknowledges the pervasive and profound role that film, television, and popular music play in the lives of many contemporary Christians. Rather than lament such a role, he suggests that Christians must be engaged with popular culture. Failure to do so, he suggests, is to fail to fulfill the biblical mandate contained in the actions of a Creator God. Nevertheless, Christians must engage popular culture with proper discernment. This book addresses how to achieve that delicate balance.

Romanowski, William D. *Pop Culture Wars: Religion and the Role of Entertainment in American Life.* Downer's Grove, IL: Intervarsity, 1996. This book is an academic analysis of the cultural conflict between religion and the entertainment industry. Romanowski presents the history of this conflict ranging from the early days of the American theater up to the present. Highly revealing, but not for the general reader.

Schultze, Quentin J., et al, eds. *Dancing in the Dark: Youth, Popular Culture and the Electronic Media.* Eerdmans, 1991. This book is a collection of essays on a variety of topics related to the role that entertainment media plays within contemporary youth culture. The authors place both adolescence and the entertainment industry within a historical and cultural context that accounts for their symbiotic need for each other. Selected essays cover topics such as rock and roll, music television, teen films, the business and artistic sides of the entertainment industry, and America's "culture of leisure."

Stevenson, Gregory. *Televised Morality: The Case of Buffy the Vampire Slayer.* Hamilton, 2004. This book examines the nature of moral discourse on television by using Buffy the Vampire Slayer as a case study. The author argues that analysis of this show's moral vision, its methods of moral reasoning, and its narrative function reveal that moral discourse on television is far more complex and sophisticated than a restrictive focus on sex, violence, and profanity allows for. The intention is to allow the analysis of this particular show to generate significant questions that then may be posed when engaging in the moral critique of other television programs.

ABOUT THE AUTHORS

JEFF W. CHILDERS is Associate Professor of Church History in the Graduate School of Theology at Abilene Christian University. After serving several years as pulpit minister with the Jeanette St. Church of Christ in Breckenridge, Texas, Jeff went to the University of Oxford where he received his D.Phil. degree. Jeff continues to enjoy frequent opportunities to preach, teach seminars, and lead workshops and retreats for churches. In his home church he teaches the high school Bible class during the school year and an elementary class during the summers.

DAVID FLEER serves as Vice President for Church Relations and Professor of Religion and Communication at Rochester College, Rochester Hills, Michigan. His devotion to ministry and preaching first found expression in a small country congregation in West Texas, was later nurtured in a Southwest Washington church and most recently shows itself in local congregations throughout metropolitan Detroit and the Midwest. David's work is characterized as a thoughtful and passionate attempt to walk afresh in the world imagined in Scripture so that disciples can experience the reality of the gospel.

RANDY HARRIS has taught at Abilene Christian University for seven years after ten years at David Lipscomb University. He was the pulpit minister for nine years at the Donelson Church of Christ in Nashville, and for two years at the S.11th and Willis Church of Christ in Abilene. He earned a certificate in Spiritual Direction from the 2-year program of the Shalem Institute and completed a 40-day contemplative prayer retreat in the Carmalite Tradition. He speaks widely for churches and conferences across the country.

MARK LOVE is Assistant Professor of Ministry and Director of Ministry Events at Abilene Christian University. His duties include directing the annual Bible Lectureship and Elderlink Northwest. Elderlink Northwest allows Mark to pursue his passion for strengthening churches in the Pacific Northwest. Before his work with ACU, Mark devoted 17 years to full-time ministry, the last 11 as Minister of the Word for the East County Church of Christ, Gresham, Oregon. His work there helped East County develop new elder role expectations that focused on the elder as a spiritual guide.

RANDY LOWRY was appointed president of Lipscomb University in Nashville, Tennessee, in September 2005. Since 1986 he was professor of law at Pepperdine University in Malibu, California, and was the founder of the nationally-recognized Straus Institute for Dispute Resolution. Through his work at the Straus Institute, Lowry has assisted many churches and individuals in resolving church-related disputes. He served as an elder at the Conejo Valley Church of Christ in Thousand Oaks, California, and has been a regular public speaker at Bible lectureships and conferences around the country.

RUBEL SHELLY served for twenty-seven years as the Preaching Minister for the Family of God at Woodmont Hills in Nashville, Tennessee. Rubel is a community leader, working with Habitat for Humanity, American Red Cross, and Nashville Public Schools. Congregational missionary work has taken him to Africa, Central America and Eastern Europe. He is currently active in helping shape the theology, lifestyle, and leadership skills of young ministers at Rochester College. In a phrase, Rubel spends his life preaching what he practices.

CHARLES SIBURT serves as Vice President for Church Relations and Frazer Professor of Church Enrichment at Abilene Christian University where he also directs the Doctor of Ministry program. Some describe him as "the church doctor" because of his ministry to churches and church leaders focusing on healthy, mature leadership. He founded the Elder-Link ministry in 2000 to equip elders and leads the Minister Support Network to encourage ministers. His interests also include constructive conflict management and redemptive pastoral ministry.

GREG STEVENSON teaches New Testament and Greek at Rochester College, Rochester Hills, Michigan. In the early nineties, he preached three years for the Marks Church of Christ in Marks, MS and continues to preach in various churches throughout Michigan. However, he finds that the ministry of teaching is where he has best been able to serve the church. He has a special interest in the church and popular media and has recently authored *Televised Morality: The Case of Buffy the Vampire Slayer*.

DAVID WRAY has served twenty years as a Highland Church of Christ shepherd, and has spent twenty years in congregational ministry. Becoming a full-time teacher at Abilene Christian University in 1990, he currently teaches ministry to undergraduate and graduate students. He earned his undergraduate and master's degrees at ACU, and his doctorate of religious education from Temple Baptist Theological Seminary.

A practical guide to the spiritual life

Living God's Love:
An Invitation to Christian Spirituality

176 pages, $12.99 · ISBN 0-9748441-2-8

by Gary Holloway & Earl Lavender

A simple, practical introduction
to the classic spiritual disciplines.
A wonderful tool for study groups,
prayer groups, and classes.

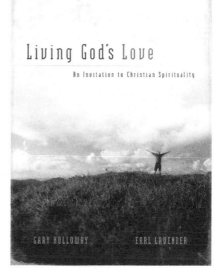

"*This profoundly simple book grounds the practices of spiritual*
maturing in a sound theology of relation in and with God. The result is
not a simple formula for instant spirituality but healthy food for the soul."

RANDY HARRIS, ABILENE CHRISTIAN UNIVERSITY

"*Our world is hungry for a life-giving way of life. That is what*
Jesus offered—and offers still. Living God's Love *makes that way*
real and alive and accessible to real-world people."

JOHN ORTBERG, AUTHOR OF *THE LIFE YOU'VE ALWAYS WANTED*

Available through your favorite bookstore
Or call toll free 1·877·816·4455

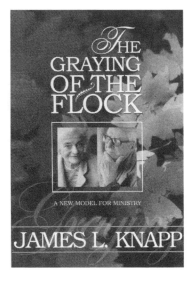